Better Homes and Gardens®

One-Dish Microwave Meals

Our seal assures you that every recipe in *One-Dish Microwave Meals*
has been tested in the Better Homes and Gardens® Test Kitchen.
This means that each recipe is practical and reliable,
and meets our high standards of taste appeal.

BETTER HOMES AND GARDENS® BOOKS
Editor: Gerald M. Knox
Art Director: Ernest Shelton
Managing Editor: David A. Kirchner
Copy and Production Editors: Marsha Jahns,
    Mary Helen Schiltz, Carl Voss, David A. Walsh

Food and Nutrition Editor: Nancy Byal
Department Head—Cook Books: Sharyl Heiken
Associate Department Heads: Sandra Granseth,
    Rosemary C. Hutchinson, Elizabeth Woolever
Senior Food Editors: Julia Malloy, Marcia Stanley,
    Joyce Trollope
Associate Food Editors: Barbara Atkins, Linda Foley,
    Linda Henry, Lynn Hoppe, Jill Johnson, Mary Jo Plutt,
    Maureen Powers, Martha Schiel
Recipe Development Editor: Marion Viall
Test Kitchen Director: Sharon Stilwell
Test Kitchen Photo Studio Director: Janet Pittman
Test Kitchen Home Economists: Jean Brekke, Kay Cargill,
    Marilyn Cornelius, Jennifer Darling, Maryellyn Krantz,
    Lynelle Munn, Dianna Nolin, Marge Steenson,
    Cynthia Volcko

Associate Art Directors: Linda Ford Vermie, Neoma Alt West,
    Randall Yontz
Assistant Art Directors: Lynda Haupert, Harijs Priekulis,
    Tom Wegner
Senior Graphic Designers: Alisann Dixon, Mike Eagleton,
    Lyne Neymeyer
Graphic Designers: Mike Burns, Sally Cooper, Deb Miner,
    Stan Sams, Darla Whipple-Frain

Vice President, Editorial Director: Doris Eby
Executive Director, Editorial Services: Duane L. Gregg

Senior Vice President, General Manager: Fred Stines
Director of Publishing: Robert B. Nelson
Vice President, Retail Marketing: Jamie Martin
Vice President, Direct Marketing: Arthur Heydendael

ONE-DISH MICROWAVE MEALS
Editor: Lynn Hoppe
Copy and Production Editor: David A. Walsh
Graphic Designer: Mike Eagleton
Electronic Text Processor: Donna Russell
Contributing Photographers: Mike Dieter; M. Jensen
    Photography, Inc.
Food Stylists: Jill Mead, Janet Pittman, Maria Rolandelli

On the cover: Bouillabaisse (see recipe, page 60).

Contents

4   **A Whole in One**
A good look at making one-dish meals
in the microwave oven.

8   **Favorites with Flair**
Fun ways with best-loved meals from around the world.

18   **Hurry-Up Square Meals**
Suppers that are ready in 30 minutes or less.

26   **Make Now, Serve Later**
Fix-'em-and-forget-'em main dishes.

34   **Shortcut to Stardom**
Shortcutting tricks for winning results.

42   **Operation Deep Freeze**
Delicious ways to build on versatile meat bases.

52   **Fit for a King**
Company-special one-dish meals.
Menu: Christmas Eve Dinner for Four

62   **Just Loafin'**
Meals-in-one served sandwich-style.

68   **Filled to the Brim**
Vegetable winners, any way you stuff 'em.

74   **Play It Again**
Leftovers to look forward to.

79   **Index**

Chicken Paella
(see recipe, page 9)

A Whole in One

For the busy cook, *One-Dish Microwave Meals* can be a stroke of genius. And to take genius one step further, here's a book chock-full of delicious one-dish-meal recipes—all prepared in the microwave oven!

Think for a minute about why you like one-dish meals and microwave cooking. If easy menu planning, speedy cooking, and no-fuss cleanup come to mind, then *One-Dish Microwave Meals* is for you. Each recipe is a complete meal in itself or with the simple addition of a salad or bread. What a great way to solve your what's-for-dinner dilemma!

Delicious meals from this book are winners in another way. Because you prepare them in the microwave oven they're ready in a flash. And after dinner, your cleanup crew will appreciate recipes that you can often mix, cook, and serve in one dish.

Look inside. You'll find loads of easy microwave recipes and tips that'll make you a timesaving genius.

Your Microwave Oven

Cooking like a pro in your microwave oven depends on getting a good handle on the basics. Here are a few tips to get you started.

Variable Power

When microwave ovens first appeared on the market, they were either "on" or "off" with no in between. Today, microwave ovens have variable power with many different settings.

Power settings and the percent of power assigned to the settings vary from brand to brand of microwave oven. For ovens with numbered settings, just multiply the number of the setting by ten to get the percent of power. So, a setting of five corresponds to 50% power.

For microwave ovens with named settings, such as "high," "medium," "defrost," or "roast," check your owner's manual or try this easy test to determine the percent of power.

A few minutes to test your oven once will save you frustrations later.

In a four-cup measure combine one cup cold water and eight ice cubes, then stir for one minute. Pour one cup of the water into a one-cup measure. Micro-cook the one cup water, uncovered, on the highest setting till it reaches a full boil, about three to four minutes. Check the timing carefully, then discard the water and allow the cup to return to room temperature. Repeat with fresh water and ice, using the setting you wish to test. If the water boils in about twice the time of your highest setting, the setting is 50% power. If the water boils in *less* than twice the time, the setting is higher than 50% power; if the water boils in more than twice the time, the setting is lower than 50% power.

Although, you'll find that most recipes in this book call for a 100% power setting, some do call for other settings. If your oven has only one power setting other than 100% power, test it, as described above. If you find that the setting is higher than 50% power, don't use your oven for recipes requiring 50% power or less. But if you find that your oven's setting is less than 50% power, use the oven only in place of powers 50% and below and plan on the food taking the maximum time or a little longer to cook.

Microwave Wattage

Because all microwave ovens do not have the same power, check the wattage listed on the oven and in the owner's manual. We tested our recipes in 600- to 700-watt ovens. If your microwave oven differs, use your owner's manual as a guide for cooking times.

Your Microwave Cookware

One of the big pluses of microwave cooking is that you often can mix, cook, and serve in the same container. But how do you know which utensils work best?

Dishes or utensils labeled "microwave-safe" or "suitable for microwaving" will work well in your microwave oven. When the dish isn't labeled, you'll need to decide what material the dish is made of, and check this list to see if it's microwave-safe.

Metal. Beware. Your owner's manual will tell you whether you can use metal in your oven. Even if you can use metal, use it only in small amounts in proportion to the amount of food you're cooking. That's because metal reflects microwave energy. Also never allow

metal to touch the sides or top of your oven during cooking. It could damage your oven.

Glass, china, or pottery. You can probably use many of the glass, china, or pottery dishes you already own. To find out which ones work, pour ½ cup water into a glass measure. Set the measure inside or beside the dish you want to test. Micro-cook on 100% power (HIGH) for one minute. If the water is warm but the dish stays cool, you may use the dish for microwave cooking. If the water is warm and the dish is lukewarm, you may use the dish for heating food. If the water stays cool and the dish is hot, don't use the dish for microwaving.

Also, don't use a dish or plate that has metallic trim or a metallic signature on the bottom.

Paper. You can use paper products in the microwave oven, but limit the cooking time to 4 minutes (10 minutes for frozen foods). Never use a paper dish with very small quantities of food (less than ¼ cup total) because the dish could catch fire. Use only white paper products. Dyes may bleed or be toxic.

Plastics. Most plastics, except melamine, are fine for microwave cooking. Because plastics vary in the food temperatures they can withstand, be sure to follow the manufacturer's directions. Don't use plastic food storage containers, such as ice cream or margarine tubs. They could melt.

Blaze-of-Glory Chili

1 pound ground beef 1 medium onion, chopped (½ cup) 1 small green pepper, seeded and chopped (½ cup) 1 clove garlic, minced	● Crumble ground beef into a 2-quart casserole, then stir in onion, green pepper, and garlic. Micro-cook, covered, on 100% power (HIGH) 5 to 6 minutes or till beef is done, stirring once to break up meat. Drain.
1 15-ounce can red kidney beans, drained 1 14½-ounce can tomatoes, cut up 1 10¾-ounce can condensed tomato soup 2 teaspoons chili powder 1 to 1½ teaspoons ground red pepper (optional) ⅛ teaspoon pepper 1 bay leaf	● Stir in kidney beans; *undrained* tomatoes; soup; chili powder; red pepper, if desired; pepper; and bay leaf. Micro-cook, covered, on 100% power (HIGH) 5 minutes; stir. Reduce power to 50% (MEDIUM). Micro-cook, covered, 20 minutes, stirring twice. Remove bay leaf. Makes 4 or 5 servings.

Attention stout-hearted chili fans. Here's a fiery version you can spice up or down to suit your taste. To give your mouth a break from the spiciness that builds with every spoonful, add a topper such as crushed crackers, shredded cheese, chopped carrot, sour cream, chopped green pepper, alfalfa sprouts, or chopped fresh tomato.

It's-a-Spicy-Spaghetti Casserole

5 ounces spaghetti 1 pound bulk Italian sausage 1 medium onion, chopped 1 stalk celery, thinly sliced 1 clove garlic, minced 1 15-ounce can tomato-herb sauce 1 4-ounce can sliced mushrooms, drained 2 teaspoons chili powder ¼ teaspoon crushed red pepper	● Cook spaghetti according to package directions. Drain. Meanwhile, crumble sausage into a 1½-quart casserole, then stir in onion, celery, and garlic. Micro-cook, covered, on 100% power (HIGH) 5 to 6 minutes or till sausage is no longer pink and onion is tender, stirring once. Drain. Stir in tomato-herb sauce, mushrooms, chili powder, and pepper.
1 cup shredded mozzarella cheese (4 ounces) 2 tablespoons snipped parsley (optional)	● Layer *half* of the spaghetti in a 10x6x2-inch baking dish, then top with *half* of the sausage mixture. Repeat layers. Cover with vented clear plastic wrap. Micro-cook on 100% power (HIGH) 8 to 10 minutes or till heated through, rotating the dish a half-turn once. Sprinkle with cheese. Micro-cook, uncovered, on 100% power (HIGH) 30 to 60 seconds or till cheese is melted. Sprinkle with parsley, if desired. Makes 4 to 6 servings.

Much of the spiciness in this casserole comes from the Italian sausage. Most brands have sausages ranging from mild to hot. So the spicier the sausage you choose, the spicier your casserole will be.

Chicken Paella

Pictured on page 5.

4 **chicken drumsticks
(1 pound)**
4 **ounces chorizo *or* Italian
sausage links, sliced**
1 **small sweet red *or* green
pepper, cut into ¾-inch
pieces (½ cup)**
1 **small onion, chopped
(¼ cup)**
2 **cloves garlic, minced**

● In a 2-quart casserole combine chicken, sausage, pepper pieces, onion, and garlic. Micro-cook, covered, on 100% power (HIGH) 7 minutes, stirring once. Drain. Remove mixture from casserole, then separate chicken pieces from rest of mixture. Set aside.

1 **cup hot water**
½ **cup long-grain rice**
1 **teaspoon instant chicken
bouillon granules**
⅛ **teaspoon thread saffron,
crushed**
**Few dashes bottled hot
pepper sauce (optional)**
2 **medium carrots, thinly
sliced (1 cup)**

● In the same casserole stir together water, *uncooked* rice, bouillon granules, saffron, and, if desired, hot pepper sauce. Micro-cook, covered, on 100% power (HIGH) 4 to 5 minutes or till boiling. Stir in sausage mixture and carrots. Arrange chicken atop. Micro-cook, covered, on 50% power (MEDIUM) 15 minutes or till rice is tender, rotating the casserole once.

1 **cup frozen peas**
1 **4½-ounce can shrimp,
rinsed and drained**
¼ **cup pitted ripe olives,
sliced**
6 **cherry tomatoes, halved,
or 1 small tomato, cut
into thin wedges**
Lemon wedges (optional)

● Thaw peas (see tip, page 17). Arrange peas, shrimp, and olives atop chicken. Top with tomatoes. Micro-cook, covered, on 100% power (HIGH) about 2 minutes or till heated through. To serve, toss gently together. Garnish with lemon wedges, if desired. Serves 4.

In Spain, anything goes when it comes to paella (pronounced *pah-A-yah*). Inlanders use sausage, ham, chicken, and vegetables. Spaniards who live on the coast, however, are more likely to opt for shrimp, clams, lobster, and mussels with their vegetables. Our version combines the best of both—it has sausage, chicken, shrimp, and vegetables.

Zucchini Lasagna

3 medium zucchini, sliced lengthwise ¼ inch thick 2 tablespoons water	● Place zucchini and water in a 10x6x2-inch baking dish, then cover with vented clear plastic wrap. Micro-cook on 100% power (HIGH) 4 to 6 minutes or till zucchini is crisp-tender, rearranging zucchini once. Drain well, then pat dry with a paper towel. Set aside.
1 pound bulk Italian sausage 1 small onion, chopped ½ of a 15½-ounce can (1 cup) meatless spaghetti sauce ⅓ cup ready-to-cook couscous	● Crumble sausage into a 1½-quart casserole, then stir in onion. Micro-cook, covered, on 100% power (HIGH) 4½ to 5½ minutes or till the sausage is no longer pink and onion is tender, stirring once to break up sausage. Drain off fat. Stir in the spaghetti sauce and couscous.
1 slightly beaten egg ¾ cup low-fat cottage cheese 2 tablespoons grated Parmesan cheese 1 cup shredded mozzarella cheese (4 ounces)	● In a small bowl combine egg, cottage cheese, and Parmesan cheese. Arrange *half* of the zucchini in the 10x6x2-inch baking dish. Top with egg mixture, then *half* of the sausage mixture. Top with remaining zucchini and sausage mixture. Cover with vented clear plastic wrap. Micro-cook on 100% power (HIGH) 8 to 10 minutes or till heated through, rotating the dish a half-turn twice. Sprinkle mozzarella cheese atop. Let stand, uncovered, for 5 minutes. Makes 6 servings.

Surprise, no pasta! Instead of noodles you use zucchini cut into long, thin strips. Remember to thoroughly drain the precooked zucchini on paper towels so it doesn't water out during cooking.

Ye New Irish Stew

1 pound boneless lamb, cut into ¾-inch pieces 1 medium onion, cut into thin wedges 1 tablespoon instant beef bouillon granules ½ teaspoon dried thyme, crushed ¼ teaspoon dried basil, crushed 1 bay leaf 2 medium potatoes, peeled and quartered 3 medium carrots, sliced ½ inch thick	● In a 3-quart casserole stir together the lamb, onion, bouillon granules, thyme, basil, 1¾ cups *water,* and ½ teaspoon *salt.* Add bay leaf. Micro-cook, covered, on 100% power (HIGH) 7 to 8 minutes or till bubbly; stir. Reduce power to 50% (MEDIUM). Micro-cook, covered, 20 minutes, stirring after 10 minutes. Stir in the potatoes and sliced carrots. Micro-cook, covered, on 50% power (MEDIUM) about 20 minutes or till lamb is done and vegetables are crisp-tender, stirring once. Remove bay leaf.
1 tablespoon cornstarch 1 tablespoon cold water	● Stir together cornstarch and water, then stir into lamb mixture. Micro-cook, uncovered, on 100% power (HIGH) 2 to 3 minutes or till thickened and bubbly, stirring once. Reduce power to 50% (MEDIUM). Micro-cook, uncovered, 2 minutes, stirring every minute. Serves 4.

Irish peasants originally used goat meat in this hearty stew. Our contemporary version calls for lamb.

Zesty Beef Stroganoff

2 pounds boneless beef round steak 2 medium onions, chopped 1 cup water 2 tablespoons cooking oil 2 cloves garlic, minced	● Partially freeze beef. Thinly bias-slice into bite-size strips. In a 3-quart casserole combine beef, onions, water, oil, and garlic. Micro-cook, covered, on 100% power (HIGH) 5 minutes; stir. Reduce power to 50% (MEDIUM). Micro-cook, covered, 22 to 24 minutes or till beef is tender, stirring after 12 minutes. Skim off fat.
½ cup chili sauce 1 tablespoon paprika 1 tablespoon chili powder 2 teaspoons seasoned salt 1 teaspoon soy sauce 1 8-ounce carton dairy sour cream 3 tablespoons all-purpose flour 1 8-ounce can sliced mushrooms, drained Hot cooked noodles Snipped chives (optional)	● Stir in the chili sauce, paprika, chili powder, seasoned salt, soy sauce, and ¾ cup *water.* Micro-cook, covered, on 100% power (HIGH) about 4 minutes or till heated through. Combine sour cream and flour. Gradually add about *1 cup* of the hot mixture to the sour cream, then return all to the casserole. Stir in the mushrooms. Micro-cook, uncovered, on 100% power (HIGH) about 6 minutes or till thickened and bubbly, stirring once. Serve over noodles. Sprinkle chives atop, if desired. Makes 8 to 10 servings.

For beef stroganoff with a kick, try our version. We've added chili sauce, chili powder, and soy sauce.

Faux Polish Hunter's Stew

½ **pound boneless pork, cut into ½-inch cubes** 1 **medium onion, chopped (½ cup)** ½ **pound fully cooked Polish sausage, sliced ½ inch thick**	● In a 2-quart casserole combine pork and onion. Micro-cook, covered, on 100% power (HIGH) 3½ minutes, stirring once. Add sausage. Micro-cook, covered, on 100% power (HIGH) 1½ minutes. Drain well.
½ **cup water** ¼ **cup dry red wine** ½ **teaspoon salt** ½ **teaspoon instant beef bouillon granules** ¼ **teaspoon ground allspice** **Dash pepper** 1 **bay leaf**	● Stir in water, wine, salt, bouillon granules, allspice, and pepper. Add bay leaf. Micro-cook, covered, on 100% power (HIGH) 5 minutes; stir. Reduce power to 50% (MEDIUM). Micro-cook, covered, 5 minutes, stirring once. Remove bay leaf.
1½ **cups shredded cabbage** 1 **8-ounce can sauerkraut, rinsed and drained** 1 **7½-ounce can tomatoes, cut up**	● Stir in the cabbage, sauerkraut, and *undrained* tomatoes. Micro-cook, covered, on 50% power (MEDIUM) 15 minutes, stirring once.
1 **medium apple, chopped (1 cup)** 1 **4½-ounce jar sliced mushrooms, drained**	● Stir in the apple and mushrooms. Micro-cook, covered, on 50% power (MEDIUM) 5 to 10 minutes or till pork is no longer pink and cabbage is tender, stirring once.
1 **tablespoon cornstarch** 1 **tablespoon cold water**	● Combine cornstarch and water, then stir into pork mixture. Micro-cook, uncovered, on 100% power (HIGH) 1 to 2 minutes or till thickened and bubbly, stirring once. Makes 4 servings.

In Poland years ago, hungry hunters came home to a hearty helping of bigos, a stew that's the national dish. The stew varied with the takes of the day and was even made with bear meat. Because bear meat is probably hard to find in your local supermarket, we thought you might prefer using Polish sausage and pork.

Taco Casserole

1 **pound ground beef**	● Crumble the beef into a 1½-quart
1 **medium onion, chopped**	casserole, then stir in onion. Micro-cook,
(½ cup)	covered, on 100% power (HIGH) 4½ to
1 **8-ounce can tomato sauce**	5½ minutes or till done. Drain, then stir
¼ **cup water**	in tomato sauce, water, and chili powder.
1 **teaspoon chili powder**	Micro-cook, covered, on 100% power
	(HIGH) about 6 minutes or till bubbly.

1 **16-ounce can refried**	● Meanwhile, stir together beans and
beans	taco sauce. Spread in bottom of a
¼ **cup taco sauce**	12x7½x2-inch baking dish, then spread
1½ **cups shredded Monterey**	the meat mixture atop. Micro-cook,
Jack cheese (6 ounces)	uncovered, on 100% power (HIGH) 7
5 **taco or tostado shells,**	to 9 minutes or till heated through.
coarsely crushed	Top with cheese. Micro-cook,
1 **cup shredded lettuce**	uncovered, on 100% power (HIGH)
1 **small tomato, chopped**	about 1 minute or till cheese is melted.
(¼ cup) (optional)	Top with crushed taco or tostado
¼ **cup sliced green onion**	shells and lettuce. If desired, top with
(optional)	tomato, green onion, olives, and avocado
¼ **cup sliced pitted ripe**	dip. Makes 6 servings.
olives (optional)	
1 **6-ounce container frozen**	
avocado dip (optional)	

Refried beans aren't really fried twice. They're pinto beans cooked with tomatoes, onion, chili pepper, and seasonings, then mashed and fried.

Macaroni and Beer Cheese

1 **cup elbow macaroni**	● Prepare macaroni according to
¼ **cup finely chopped onion**	package directions. Drain and set aside.
¼ **cup finely chopped green**	In a 1½-quart casserole micro-cook
pepper	onion, pepper, and butter or margarine,
2 **tablespoons butter *or***	uncovered, on 100% power (HIGH) 2
margarine	to 3 minutes or till onion is tender.

4 **teaspoons all-purpose**	● Stir in flour, bouillon granules, and
flour	pepper, then stir in milk all at once.
1 **teaspoon instant beef**	Micro-cook, uncovered, on 100% power
bouillon granules	(HIGH) 3 to 4 minutes or till thickened
¼ **teaspoon pepper**	and bubbly, stirring every minute.
¾ **cup milk**	

1½ **cups shredded American**	● Stir in cheese, beer, and hot pepper
cheese (6 ounces)	sauce. Stir in macaroni and tomato.
¼ **cup beer**	Micro-cook, covered, on 70% power
Few dashes bottled hot	(MEDIUM-HIGH) 4 to 5 minutes or till
pepper sauce	heated through. Sprinkle with parsley
1 **medium tomato, chopped**	and top with tomato wedges, if desired.
(½ cup)	Makes 3 servings.
1 **tablespoon snipped**	
parsley (optional)	
1 **medium tomato, cut into**	
thin wedges (optional)	

Macaroni and cheese gets a new lease on life with this spicy, beer-cheese sauce. It'll set your palate hoppin'!

Chicken Couscous

1 **medium onion, thinly sliced and separated into rings** 2 **medium carrots, thinly sliced (1 cup)** 2 **tablespoons butter** *or* **margarine** 2 **cloves garlic, minced**	● Place the onion, carrots, butter or margarine, and garlic in a 12x7½x 2-inch baking dish. Cover with vented clear plastic wrap. Micro-cook on 100% power (HIGH) 5 minutes, stirring once. Remove from the baking dish and set aside.
6 **chicken thighs** 2 **teaspoons chili powder** ¾ **teaspoon ground ginger** ¾ **teaspoon ground cumin**	● In the same baking dish arrange chicken, skin side down, with meatiest portions toward outside of the dish. Cover with vented clear plastic wrap. Micro-cook on 100% power (HIGH) 9 minutes, rotating the dish a half-turn after 5 minutes. Remove chicken. Drain fat. In a small bowl combine chili powder, ginger, and cumin.
1 **14½-ounce can stewed tomatoes, cut up** 1 **stalk celery, cut into 1-inch pieces** ½ **cup water**	● Return carrot mixture to the baking dish. Stir in *undrained* tomatoes, celery, water, and *half* of the spices. Arrange chicken, skin side up, in the dish with meaty portions to outside of the dish. Sprinkle remaining spices over chicken. Cover with vented clear plastic wrap. Micro-cook on 70% power (MEDIUM-HIGH) 20 to 25 minutes or till chicken is done, basting chicken and rotating the dish a half-turn every 10 minutes.
1½ **cups ready-to-cook couscous** ¼ **cup snipped parsley (optional)**	● Meanwhile, prepare couscous according to package directions. Stir in parsley, if desired. Spoon couscous onto a large platter. Arrange chicken atop. Use a slotted spoon to place vegetables atop, reserving juices. Keep warm.
2 **tablespoons cold water** 2 **tablespoons cornstarch** ½ **cup raisins** ½ **cup peanuts**	● Skim fat from reserved juices. Pour into a 4-cup glass measure. Stir together water and cornstarch. Stir into juices. Micro-cook, uncovered, on 100% power (HIGH) 2 to 3 minutes or till thickened and bubbly, stirring every minute. Stir in raisins and peanuts. Spoon atop chicken. Makes 6 servings.

Just saying the word couscous (pronounced KOO-skoos) conjures up images of exotic places. This steamed coarsely ground wheat (semolina) is typical of dishes served in Morocco, Algeria, and Tunisia. Look for couscous in your grocery or health food store.

Beef and Vegetable Carbonnade

1 **pound beef round steak** 1 **10-ounce package frozen cut broccoli** 1 **tablespoon cooking oil** 1 **small onion, cut into thin wedges**	● Partially freeze beef. Thinly bias-slice beef into bite-size strips. Thaw broccoli (see tip, below). Drain and set aside. Preheat a 10-inch microwave browning dish on 100% power (HIGH) 5 minutes. Add oil, then swirl to coat dish. Add beef and onion. Micro-cook, uncovered, on 100% power (HIGH) 5 to 6 minutes or till beef is done, stirring twice.	**A Flemish carbonnade purist would do a double take on our version of this beef and onion stew cooked in beer. Broccoli and carrot add colorful crunch. Serving the delicious concoction over noodles just takes unorthodoxy one step further.**
1 **cup beer** 2 **teaspoons brown sugar** 2 **teaspoons instant beef bouillon granules** ½ **teaspoon dried thyme, crushed** ⅛ **teaspoon cracked pepper** 2 **cloves garlic, minced** ½ **cup shredded carrot** ½ **cup water**	● Stir in beer, brown sugar, bouillon granules, thyme, pepper, and garlic. Micro-cook, covered, on 100% power (HIGH) about 7 minutes or till bubbly. Reduce power to 70% (MEDIUM-HIGH). Micro-cook, covered, about 15 minutes or till beef is tender. Stir in broccoli, carrot, and water. Micro-cook, covered, on 100% power (HIGH) 4 to 6 minutes or till broccoli is tender.	
2 **tablespoons cold water** 4 **teaspoons cornstarch** **Hot cooked noodles**	● Stir together water and cornstarch. Stir into beef mixture. Micro-cook, uncovered, on 100% power (HIGH) 2 to 3 minutes or till thickened and bubbly, stirring every minute. Serve atop noodles. Makes 4 servings.	

Thawing Vegetables in a Hurry

Your microwave oven comes in especially handy when you want to thaw 9- or 10-ounce packages of frozen vegetables quickly. Just remove the vegetables from the package and place them in a small bowl. Micro-cook, uncovered, on 30% power (MEDIUM-LOW) 8 to 11 minutes or till thawed, stirring every 3 minutes.

Sweet-and-Sour-Sauced Pork

¾ **pound boneless pork**
1 **tablespoon cooking oil**

● Thinly bias-slice pork into bite-size strips. Preheat a 10-inch microwave browning dish on 100% power (HIGH) 5 minutes. Add oil, then swirl to coat dish. Add pork. Micro-cook, uncovered, on 100% power (HIGH) 2 to 4 minutes or till no longer pink.
　Use a slotted spoon to remove pork from the browning dish, reserving juices in the dish. Set pork aside.

● **Preparation time: 20 minutes**

1 **6-ounce package frozen pea pods**
1 **cup frozen crinkle-cut carrots**

● Thaw pea pods and carrots (see tip, page 17). In juices in the browning dish micro-cook vegetables, covered, on 100% power (HIGH) 4 to 5 minutes or till crisp-tender.

Start with peach or pineapple pie filling. Then stir in some vinegar and soy sauce. You'll get plenty of sweet-and-sour flavor—the easy way!

1 **21-ounce can peach *or* pineapple pie filling**
3 **tablespoons vinegar**
3 **tablespoons soy sauce**
1 **teaspoon instant chicken bouillon granules**
　Hot cooked rice

● In a small bowl stir together pie filling, vinegar, soy sauce, and bouillon granules. Stir pie filling mixture and pork into vegetables. Micro-cook, uncovered, on 100% power (HIGH) 3 to 5 minutes or till heated through. Serve over rice. Makes 4 servings.

Corny Calico Casseroles

2 teaspoons butter *or* margarine ½ cup cornbread stuffing mix	● In a small bowl micro-cook butter or margarine, uncovered, on 100% power (HIGH) 30 to 40 seconds or till melted. Toss with stuffing mix, then set aside.
1 cup frozen whole kernel corn ½ of a small sweet red *or* green pepper, chopped 2 tablespoons sliced green onion 1 tablespoon butter *or* margarine	● In a 1-quart casserole combine corn, pepper, green onion, and butter or margarine. Micro-cook, covered, on 100% power (HIGH) about 3 minutes or till pepper is crisp-tender.
2 eggs ¼ cup milk ¼ teaspoon Worcestershire sauce Dash pepper ¼ pound cooked Polish sausage, chopped ½ cup shredded Swiss cheese (2 ounces)	● In a 2-cup measure beat together eggs, milk, Worcestershire, and pepper slightly with a fork. Stir egg mixture, sausage, and cheese into corn mixture. Spoon into two 15-ounce casseroles. Sprinkle stuffing mixture on top. Micro-cook, uncovered, on 100% power (HIGH) 6 to 7 minutes or till almost set. Let stand 2 minutes. Serves 2.

● **Preparation time:
20 minutes**

One of our food editors suggested the title for this dish. "The bits of corn, pepper, and sausage make these look like calico casseroles," she said.

Chilies and Cheese Rice

1 medium onion, chopped
　　(½ cup)
1 small green pepper, cut
　　into ¾-inch pieces
1 tablespoon butter *or*
　　margarine
1 clove garlic, minced

● In a 1½-quart casserole combine the onion, pepper, butter or margarine, and garlic. Micro-cook, covered, on 100% power (HIGH) 2 minutes.

● **Preparation time:
　30 minutes**

When time's ticking away, shredding cheese can be a real hassle. Plan ahead for those precious moments. When you have time, shred a block of cheese all at once. Then store it, tightly wrapped, in ½- or 1-cup portions for a week in the refrigerator or for six months in the freezer.

1 15-ounce can red kidney
　　beans, drained
1 14½-ounce can tomatoes,
　　cut up
1 cup quick-cooking rice
1 4-ounce can diced green
　　chili peppers, drained
1 teaspoon chili powder
1 cup shredded American
　　cheese (4 ounces)
1 medium tomato, thinly
　　sliced and halved
　　(optional)
　Dairy sour cream
　　(optional)

● Stir in kidney beans, *undrained* tomatoes, *uncooked* rice, chili peppers, and chili powder. Micro-cook, covered, on 100% power (HIGH) 14 to 16 minutes or till rice is tender, stirring twice. Stir in cheese. If desired, arrange tomato slices atop rice mixture. Micro-cook, covered, on 100% power (HIGH) 1 minute more. Serve with sour cream, if desired. Makes 4 servings.

Letting Off Steam

Covering foods makes microwave cooking even faster because the steam that builds up under the cover helps cook the food. Covering also keeps the food from drying out and eliminates spattering.

Microwave-safe clear plastic wrap is a great cover for dishes you cook in the microwave oven. Microwave-safe plastic wraps withstand microwave temperatures well, as long as they don't come in contact with the hot food. Some plastic wraps are so good at their job, however, that they form a nearly airtight seal with the edge of the dish. To avoid a blowup when steam builds up in the dish and possible burns that may result, vent the clear plastic wrap so steam escapes. Just fold back a small area of the plastic wrap at the edge of the baking dish.

Creamed Chickaroni Casserole

1½ cups elbow macaroni
1 cup milk
1 10¾-ounce can condensed cream of mushroom soup
1½ cups frozen peas
1 6¾-ounce can chunk-style chicken *or* one 6½-ounce can tuna, drained and flaked
1 3-ounce can french-fried onions
½ cup shredded cheddar cheese (2 ounces)
1 2-ounce jar diced pimiento, drained

● Prepare macaroni according to package directions. Drain and keep warm. Meanwhile, in a 2-quart casserole stir milk into soup. Stir in peas, chicken or tuna, *half* of the onions, cheese, and pimiento. Micro-cook, covered, on 100% power (HIGH) about 9 minutes or till heated through, stirring once.

● **Preparation time: 25 minutes**

Cooking pasta in your microwave oven takes about as much time as cooking it conventionally. That's why we suggest you cook the macaroni on your range top. Meanwhile, use your microwave oven where it counts the most—to shortcut cooking the chicken or tuna mixture.

½ cup shredded cheddar cheese (2 ounces)

● Stir in macaroni. Arrange remaining onions around edge of the casserole. Sprinkle cheese in center. Micro-cook, uncovered, on 100% power (HIGH) 1 to 1½ minutes or till cheese is melted. Makes 4 to 6 servings.

Chili-Mac Casserole

¾ cup medium shell macaroni
½ pound ground beef
1 stalk celery, thinly sliced
1 small onion, chopped
1½ teaspoons chili powder

● Cook macaroni according to package directions. Drain. Meanwhile, crumble beef into a 1½-quart casserole, then stir in celery and onion. Micro-cook, covered, on 100% power (HIGH) 3½ to 4½ minutes or till beef is done and onion is tender, stirring once to break up meat. Drain. Stir chili powder into beef mixture. Micro-cook, covered, on 100% power (HIGH) 1 minute.

● **Preparation time: 25 minutes**

Effortless menu planning can become second nature. Just keep in mind that the flavors, textures, and temperatures of the foods you choose should complement each other. For instance, this mildly spicy casserole needs a cool, crunchy contrast, such as celery or carrot sticks. Now that's simple!

1 8½-ounce can whole kernel corn, drained
1 8-ounce can red kidney beans, drained
1 8-ounce can tomato sauce
¼ teaspoon salt
¼ cup shredded cheddar cheese (1 ounce)

● Stir in macaroni, corn, kidney beans, tomato sauce, and salt. Micro-cook, uncovered, on 70% power (MEDIUM-HIGH) about 10 minutes or till heated through, stirring once. Sprinkle cheese atop casserole. Makes 4 servings.

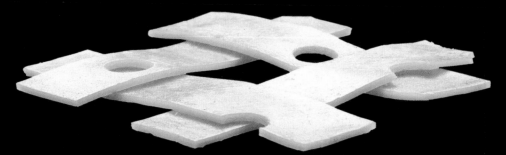

Ham-and-Rye Strata

2 slices day-old rye bread, cut into bite-size cubes
1 cup diced fully cooked ham
½ cup shredded Swiss cheese (2 ounces)
½ cup milk
2 beaten eggs
¼ teaspoon caraway seed (optional)
⅛ teaspoon dry mustard
⅛ teaspoon pepper

● Combine bread and ham. Divide *half* of the bread and ham between 2 individual round 10-ounce casseroles. Reserve remaining bread and ham. Sprinkle cheese atop ham and bread. Micro-cook milk, uncovered, on 100% power (HIGH) 1 to 2 minutes or till hot (180°), but *not* boiling. In a 1-cup measure gradually stir milk into eggs. Stir in caraway seed, if desired; dry mustard; and pepper.

● **Preparation time: 20 minutes**

For a strata to be a strata, you must have the layers. Usually stratas include a layer of bread and sliced or shredded cheese bound together with a sauce or egg mixture.

1 slice Swiss cheese, cut into 8 narrow strips (1 ounce)

● Pour *half* of the milk mixture over cheese in each casserole. Top with remaining bread and ham. Micro-cook, covered, on 50% power (MEDIUM) 6 to 8 minutes or till almost set, rotating twice. Arrange cheese atop. Let stand 5 minutes. Serves 2.

Greek Lamb and Cheese Casserole

4 ounces medium noodles
  (3 cups)
1 pound ground lamb
2 stalks celery, thinly sliced
  (1 cup)

- Prepare noodles according to package directions. Drain. Meanwhile, crumble lamb into a 2-quart casserole, then stir in celery. Micro-cook, covered, on 100% power (HIGH) 5 to 6 minutes or till lamb is done, stirring once to break up lamb. Drain off fat.

1 10¾-ounce can
  condensed cream of
  mushroom soup
1 cup crumbled feta
  cheese or shredded
  mozzarella cheese
  (4 ounces)
½ cup sliced pitted ripe
  olives
½ cup plain yogurt
⅓ cup milk
¼ to ½ teaspoon dried
  oregano, crushed
2 tablespoons snipped
  parsley
1 medium tomato, cut
  into thin wedges

- Stir the cream of mushroom soup, feta or mozzarella cheese, olives, yogurt, milk, oregano, and ⅛ teaspoon *pepper* into the lamb mixture. Stir in the cooked noodles. Micro-cook the lamb mixture, covered, on 100% power (HIGH) 6 to 8 minutes or till heated through, stirring twice. Sprinkle snipped parsley atop the lamb mixture. Arrange the tomato wedges atop. Makes 6 servings.

- **Preparation time:
  25 minutes**

The only sure way to know if the noodles are done is to taste them. If they are tender but still slightly firm and no longer taste starchy, they're done. The Italians call this stage *al dente,* meaning "to the tooth." Immediately drain the noodles to prevent further cooking.

Organize for Speedy Suppers

Organization is the key to getting meals ready on the double. First, arrange your kitchen so you can find things quickly. (Another hint: Stock duplicates of often-used utensils to cut down on midrecipe dishwashing.) Second, plan meals for several days and get all your groceries at once.

Third, read recipes through and assemble everything you need before starting. Finally, dovetail steps. For example, in Greek Lamb and Cheese Casserole you can cook the noodles on your range top at the same time you cook the beef in your microwave oven.

Peppered Beef

1 **10-ounce package frozen brussels sprouts**
¾ **pound beef top round steak**
1 **tablespoon cooking oil**

● Thaw brussels sprouts (see tip, page 17). Cut in half. Set aside. Thinly bias-slice beef into bite-size strips. Preheat a 10-inch microwave browning dish on 100% power (HIGH) 5 minutes. Add oil to browning dish, then swirl to coat dish. Add beef. Micro-cook, uncovered, on 100% power (HIGH) 2 to 3 minutes or till done, stirring once. Use a slotted spoon to remove beef and reserve juices in the browning dish. Set beef aside.

⅓ **cup dry sherry**
¼ **cup water**
¼ **cup soy sauce**
¾ **to 1 teaspoon crushed whole black pepper**
2 **cloves garlic, minced**
2 **medium carrots, thinly sliced (1 cup)**

● Meanwhile, in a small bowl stir together sherry, water, soy sauce, pepper, and garlic. Stir into reserved juices. Add brussels sprouts and carrots. Micro-cook, covered, on 100% power (HIGH) 5 to 7 minutes or till vegetables are crisp-tender.

2 **tablespoons cold water**
2 **teaspoons cornstarch**
   Hot cooked noodles *or* spaetzle

● Stir water into cornstarch. Stir into vegetable mixture. Micro-cook, uncovered, on 100% power (HIGH) 2 to 4 minutes or till thickened and bubbly, stirring every minute. Stir in beef. Micro-cook, uncovered, on 100% power (HIGH) 2 to 3 minutes or till heated through. Serve over noodles or spaetzle. Makes 4 servings.

● **Preparation time: 30 minutes**

For easier slicing, put the meat in the freezer until it's firm but not hard—about 45 minutes should do. If the meat is already frozen, just partially thaw.

To bias-slice, hold a sharp knife or cleaver at a 45-degree angle to the cutting board while you thinly slice the meat. If the meat slices are large, cut them into bite-size pieces.

Salmon-Noodle Bake

4 ounces medium whole wheat *or* regular noodles	● Prepare noodles according to package directions. Drain. Meanwhile, in a 1½-quart casserole micro-cook onion, green pepper, and butter or margarine, covered, on 100% power (HIGH) 2 to 3 minutes or till onion is tender.
¼ cup chopped onion	
¼ cup chopped green pepper	
1 tablespoon butter *or* margarine	

1 3-ounce package cream cheese, softened	● Add softened cream cheese to the onion mixture, stirring till melted. Stir in cottage cheese, Parmesan cheese, milk, prepared mustard, Worcestershire sauce, and basil. Add the cooked noodles, salmon, and pimiento to mixture, then toss well to coat. Turn into a 10x6x2-inch baking dish. Cover the baking dish and refrigerate for 3 to 24 hours.
1 cup cream-style cottage cheese	
¼ cup grated Parmesan cheese	
¼ cup milk	
1 teaspoon prepared mustard	
1 teaspoon Worcestershire sauce	
¼ teaspoon dried basil, crushed	
1 7¾-ounce can salmon, drained, flaked, and skin and bones removed	
2 tablespoons sliced pimiento, drained and chopped	

Next time you buy canned salmon, remember this rule of thumb: the redder the flesh, the higher the price. Salmon varieties, from pinkest (least expensive) to reddest (most expensive), are chum, pink, silver, king, chinook, and sockeye. Because you'll mix the ingredients together in Salmon-Noodle Bake, the least expensive variety works just fine.

1 tablespoon butter *or* margarine	● Before mealtime, prepare topper by micro-cooking butter or margarine, uncovered, on 100% power (HIGH) 30 to 40 seconds or till melted. Toss with crackers. Sprinkle cracker mixture around outer edge of noodle mixture. Micro-cook, uncovered, on 100% power (HIGH) 12 to 15 minutes or till heated through, rotating the dish once. If desired, garnish with parsley and tomato rose. Makes 6 servings.
8 rich round crackers, crushed	
Parsley	
Tomato rose	

Corn Bread Dumplings

⅓ cup all-purpose flour
⅓ cup yellow cornmeal
1 tablespoon sugar
1 teaspoon baking powder
¼ teaspoon salt
1 slightly beaten egg yolk
¼ cup milk
2 tablespoons cooking oil
Choose-a-Dumpling Beef
Stew (see recipe,
page 30)

● In a medium bowl stir together flour, cornmeal, sugar, baking powder, and salt.
Combine egg yolk, milk, and oil, then add to flour mixture, stirring with a fork only till combined.
Drop cornmeal mixture from a tablespoon directly onto bubbly stew to make 4 dumplings. Micro-cook, uncovered, on 100% power (HIGH) 3½ to 4 minutes or till a wooden toothpick inserted into center of dumplings comes out clean, rotating the dish twice.

When your dumpling-topped stew comes to the table, just add a beverage to make your meal complete.

Cheddar Dumplings

1 cup packaged biscuit mix
⅓ cup milk
¼ cup shredded cheddar
cheese (1 ounce)
Choose-a-Dumpling Beef
Stew (see recipe,
page 30)

● In a medium bowl stir together biscuit mix, milk, and cheese.
Drop the biscuit mixture from a tablespoon directly onto bubbly stew to make 4 dumplings. Micro-cook, uncovered, on 70% power (MEDIUM-HIGH) 5 to 8 minutes or till a wooden toothpick inserted in center of dumplings comes out clean, rotating the dish twice.

Herbed Dumplings: Prepare Cheddar Dumplings as above, *except* substitute 1 tablespoon snipped *parsley or* 1 teaspoon *dried parsley flakes* and ¾ teaspoon snipped *thyme or* ¼ teaspoon *dried thyme,* crushed, for the cheese.

Carrot Dumplings: Prepare the Cheddar Dumplings as above, *except* substitute ½ cup finely shredded *carrot* and 2 tablespoons grated *Parmesan cheese* for cheddar cheese.

Choose-a-Dumpling Beef Stew

Pictured on pages 28–29.

1 **8-ounce package frozen cut broccoli** 1 **pound boneless beef chuck steak, cut into ¾-inch cubes** 1 **medium onion, cut into thin wedges** 1 **cup water** 2 **teaspoons instant beef bouillon granules** 1 **clove garlic, minced** 1 **bay leaf** **Dash pepper**	● Thaw broccoli (see tip, page 17). Set aside. In a 2-quart casserole combine beef, onion, water, bouillon granules, garlic, bay leaf, and pepper. Micro-cook, covered, on 100% power (HIGH) about 8 minutes or till bubbly; stir. Reduce power to 50% (MEDIUM). Micro-cook, covered, 20 minutes, stirring once.
1 **8-ounce can tomato sauce** 2 **stalks celery, sliced (1 cup)** 2 **medium carrots, sliced (1 cup)** 2 **tablespoons Dijon-style mustard** ½ **teaspoon Worcestershire sauce**	● Stir in tomato sauce, celery, carrots, mustard, and Worcestershire sauce. Micro-cook, covered, on 100% power (HIGH) 5 minutes; stir. Reduce power to 50% (MEDIUM). Micro-cook, covered, 10 minutes, stirring once. Stir in broccoli. Micro-cook, covered, on 50% power (MEDIUM) 8 minutes.
2 **tablespoons cornstarch** 2 **tablespoons cold water**	● Stir together cornstarch and water. Stir into meat mixture. Micro-cook, uncovered, on 100% power (HIGH) 2 to 3 minutes or till thickened and bubbly, stirring every minute. Reduce power to 50% (MEDIUM). Micro-cook, uncovered, 2 minutes more, stirring every minute. Remove bay leaf. Cover and refrigerate for 3 to 24 hours.
Corn Bread Dumplings, Cheddar Dumplings, Herbed Dumplings, *or* Carrot Dumplings (see recipes, page 28)	● Before mealtime, micro-cook beef mixture, covered, on 100% power (HIGH) 7 to 9 minutes or till bubbly, stirring twice. Prepare dumplings as directed. Makes 4 servings.

Pick a topper, any topper among four delicious choices (see recipes, page 28). They all blossom into delectable dumplings when you cook them on top of this hearty stew.

Pork-and-Spinach Manicotti

8 manicotti shells 1 10-ounce package frozen chopped spinach	● Cook manicotti according to package directions. Drain and set aside. Thaw spinach (see tip, page 17). Drain well, pressing out excess liquid. Set aside.

To fill manicotti, spoon some of the sausage-and-cottage cheese mixture into each cooked shell. Try using a small iced tea spoon. The long handle makes it easy to get the mixture into the shells.

1 pound bulk Italian sausage
1 medium onion, chopped (½ cup)
1 clove garlic, minced
1 slightly beaten egg yolk
1 cup low-fat cottage cheese, drained
¼ cup grated Parmesan cheese
1 teaspoon dried oregano, crushed
½ teaspoon dried basil, crushed
¼ teaspoon salt

● Crumble sausage into a 1½-quart casserole, then stir in onion and garlic. Micro-cook, covered, on 100% power (HIGH) 7 to 9 minutes or till sausage is no longer pink, stirring twice. Drain. Meanwhile, in a small bowl stir together egg yolk, cottage cheese, Parmesan cheese, oregano, basil, and salt. Stir spinach and cottage cheese mixture into sausage mixture.

Spoon some of the sausage and cottage cheese mixture into *each* manicotti shell. Place in a 12x7½x 2-inch baking dish. Spoon remaining filling around edges of shells. Cover and refrigerate for 3 to 24 hours.

1 15-ounce can tomato-herb sauce
½ teaspoon sugar
2 tablespoons grated Parmesan cheese

● Before mealtime, combine tomato-herb sauce and sugar. Pour sauce mixture over shells. Cover with vented clear plastic wrap. Micro-cook on 100% power (HIGH) 12 to 15 minutes or till heated through. Sprinkle Parmesan cheese atop shells. Makes 6 servings.

Minimize work at mealtime by making your salad ahead. Wash salad ingredients and chop firm vegetables such as carrots, celery, and green peppers in advance. At mealtime, finish preparing the salad and set the table while Pork-and-Spinach Manicotti reheats.

Creole-Style Chicken

1 **medium green pepper, chopped (¾ cup)**
1 **medium onion, chopped**
1 **tablespoon butter *or* margarine**
1 **clove garlic, minced**

● In a 2-quart casserole micro-cook pepper, onion, butter or margarine, and garlic, covered, on 100% power (HIGH) 2 to 3 minutes or till onion is tender.

1 **14½-ounce can tomatoes, cut up**
1½ **cups frozen diced cooked chicken**
½ **of a 6-ounce can (⅓ cup) tomato paste**
½ **teaspoon chili powder**
¼ **teaspoon sugar**
¼ **teaspoon ground red pepper**
¼ **teaspoon dried thyme, crushed**
¼ **teaspoon cracked black pepper**

● Stir in *undrained* tomatoes, chicken, tomato paste, chili powder, sugar, ground red pepper, thyme, pepper, and ¼ teaspoon *salt*. Cover and refrigerate for 3 to 24 hours.

Hot cooked rice

● Before mealtime, micro-cook, covered, on 100% power (HIGH) 7 to 8 minutes or till heated through, stirring twice. Serve over rice. Makes 4 servings.

Creole cooks combine the best of Spanish and French cuisines, then add the fresh ingredients from Louisiana and other Gulf States—truly a melting pot of culinary influences.

Beef and Bean Paprikash

1 pound boneless beef sirloin steak **1 9-ounce package frozen cut green beans** **1 tablespoon cooking oil** **1 medium onion, chopped (½ cup)**	● Partially freeze beef. Thinly bias-slice into bite-size strips. Thaw beans (see tip, page 17). Drain and set aside. Preheat a 10-inch microwave browning dish on 100% power (HIGH) 5 minutes. Add oil, then swirl to coat dish. Add beef and onion. Micro-cook, uncovered, on 100% power (HIGH) 4½ to 5 minutes or till beef is done, stirring once.
1 cup water **2 tablespoons paprika** **½ teaspoon instant beef bouillon granules** **¼ teaspoon salt** **¼ teaspoon dried thyme, crushed** **¼ teaspoon dried rosemary, crushed** **⅛ teaspoon pepper**	● Stir together water, paprika, bouillon granules, salt, thyme, rosemary, and pepper. Stir into beef mixture. Micro-cook, covered, on 100% power (HIGH) about 5 minutes or till boiling. Reduce power to 70% (MEDIUM-HIGH). Micro-cook, covered, about 5 minutes or till beef is tender. Stir in beans. Micro-cook, covered, on 100% power (HIGH) 4 to 6 minutes or till beans are crisp-tender. Let stand, uncovered, 5 minutes. Cover and refrigerate for 3 to 24 hours.
½ cup dairy sour cream **2 tablespoons all-purpose flour** **Hot cooked noodles**	● Before mealtime, micro-cook beef mixture, covered, on 100% power (HIGH) 12 minutes, stirring once. Stir together sour cream and flour. Stir into beef mixture. Micro-cook, uncovered, on 100% power (HIGH) 2 to 4 minutes or till thickened and bubbly, stirring every minute. Serve over hot cooked noodles. Makes 4 servings.

Hungarians are particularly partial to paprika. The mild-flavored red seasoning is made from grinding dried sweet peppers.

Beer-Sauced Meatballs

1 beaten egg
1 10¾-ounce can
   condensed tomato *or*
   cheddar cheese soup
1 cup soft bread crumbs
¼ teaspoon salt
1 pound ground beef
	● In a small bowl combine egg and ¼ *cup* of the soup. Stir in bread crumbs and salt. Add ground beef and mix well. Shape into 36 meatballs. Arrange in a 12x7½x2-inch baking dish. Micro-cook, uncovered, on 100% power (HIGH) 8 to 12 minutes or till done, rearranging meatballs twice. Push meatballs to side of the dish. Drain.

½ cup beer
½ teaspoon dried oregano,
   crushed
   Dash pepper
1 medium onion, sliced and
   separated into rings
   Hot cooked noodles,
   spaetzle, *or* rice
	● Combine remaining soup, beer, oregano, and pepper. Pour soup mixture over meatballs. Add onion. Micro-cook, covered, on 100% power (HIGH) 5 to 8 minutes or till onion is just tender. Serve over hot cooked noodles, spaetzle, or rice. Makes 6 servings.

Pull out your blender to make soft bread crumbs fast. Just quarter bread slices and place a few at a time in the blender container. Cover and blend till coarsely chopped. A slice of bread makes about ¾ cup crumbs.

Cock-a-Noodle Casserole

3 ounces medium noodles
   (1½ cups)
½ cup frozen mixed
   vegetables
1 10¾-ounce can
   condensed cream of
   chicken soup
1 4-ounce package (1 cup)
   shredded cheddar
   cheese
½ cup milk
½ cup dairy sour cream
	● Prepare noodles according to package directions. Drain. Meanwhile, thaw vegetables (see tip, page 17). Drain and set aside.
	   In a 2-quart casserole combine soup, *half* of the cheese, milk, and sour cream.

1 5-ounce can chunk-style chicken, flaked	● Stir noodles, vegetables, and chicken into soup mixture. Micro-cook, covered, on 100% power (HIGH) 8 to 10 minutes or till heated through, stirring once.
¼ cup toasted wheat germ	● Sprinkle remaining cheese on top. Sprinkle with wheat germ. Micro-cook, uncovered, on 100% power (HIGH) 1 to 2 minutes or till cheese melts. Serves 4.

Make the most of available convenience products to shortcut recipes. In Cock-a-Noodle Casserole you skip a step by buying cheese that's already shredded. Look for more work-saving ingredients—such as chopped nuts, frozen chopped onion, frozen chopped green pepper, minced dried onion, and minced dried garlic— to help shortcut cooking other one-dish meals.

Mexican Corn Bread Casserole

¼ cup water 3 tablespoons butter *or* margarine 2¼ cups corn bread stuffing mix, crushed 1 slightly beaten egg	● In a medium bowl micro-cook water and butter or margarine, uncovered, on 100% power (HIGH) 45 to 60 seconds or till butter is melted. Stir in stuffing mix and egg till moistened. Turn crumb mixture into a 9-inch pie plate. Using your hands, press crumb mixture firmly against bottom and sides of pie plate, then set aside.
¾ pound ground beef ½ of a medium onion, chopped (¼ cup) 1 8-ounce can red kidney beans, drained 1 cup shredded Monterey Jack cheese with jalapeño peppers (4 ounces) ½ of an 8-ounce can (½ cup) tomato sauce 2 teaspoons chili powder	● Crumble beef into the mixing bowl, then stir in onion. Micro-cook, covered, on 100% power (HIGH) about 4 minutes or till beef is done and onion is tender, stirring once to break up beef. Drain off fat. Stir in kidney beans, cheese, tomato sauce, and chili powder. Turn meat mixture into crust.
½ cup shredded Monterey Jack cheese with jalapeño peppers (2 ounces)	● Micro-cook, uncovered, on 100% power (HIGH) 6 to 8 minutes or till heated through, rotating the dish every 3 minutes. Top with cheese. Cover and let stand 5 minutes. Makes 6 servings.

You'll breathe fire after a sample of Mexican Corn Bread Casserole. Quench the flames with a no-fuss, cooling salad of avocado or tomato halves filled with cottage cheese and topped with bottled dressing. Or, practice fire prevention by using Monterey Jack cheese without the jalapeño peppers.

Easy Cassoulet

½ **pound Italian sausage links, cut into ½-inch pieces**
2 **stalks celery, thinly sliced (1 cup)**
1 **medium onion, chopped (½ cup)**

● In a 2-quart casserole combine the sausage, celery, and onion. Micro-cook, covered, on 100% power (HIGH) 7 to 8 minutes or till sausage is no longer pink and celery is tender, stirring once to break up sausage. Drain.

1 **15-ounce can navy beans**
¼ **pound cubed fully cooked ham (¾ cup)**
¼ **cup water**
¼ **cup dry white wine**
2 **tablespoons snipped parsley**
1 **bay leaf**

● Stir in *undrained* beans, ham, water, wine, and parsley. Add bay leaf. Micro-cook, covered, on 100% power (HIGH) 6 to 8 minutes or till bubbly over entire surface, stirring twice. Remove bay leaf, then mash beans slightly. Serves 4.

Add Italian sausage to a recipe such as Easy Cassoulet and much more goes in than just the meat. Fennel, garlic, coriander, nutmeg, paprika, and sometimes red pepper are in the sausage. These built-in seasonings taste terrific and save you valuable time because you don't need to measure them.

Second-String Substitutions

When you're in a bind, ingredient substitutions make real supper savers. You may substitute:
● 2 tablespoons all-purpose flour for 1 tablespoon cornstarch (for thickening)
● ½ cup evaporated milk plus ½ cup water *or* 1 cup reconstituted nonfat dry milk (plus 2 teaspoons butter *or* margarine, if desired) for 1 cup whole milk
● ¾ cup tomato paste plus 1 cup water for 2 cups tomato sauce
● ½ cup tomato sauce plus ½ cup water for 1 cup tomato juice
● ⅛ teaspoon garlic powder *or* minced dried garlic for 1 clove garlic
● 1 teaspoon onion powder *or* 1 tablespoon minced dried onion for 1 small onion
● 1 tablespoon prepared mustard for 1 teaspoon dry mustard

Salami-Vegetable Bake

The food processor and microwave oven make a great timesaving team. For recipes such as Salami Vegetable Bake, prepare vegetables quickly in the food processor to get uniform pieces that cook evenly in the microwave oven.

4	medium potatoes, peeled and sliced
2	carrots, sliced (1 cup)
1	medium onion, sliced
⅓	cup water
¼	teaspoon minced dried garlic
3	cups shredded cabbage

● In a 2-quart casserole combine the potatoes, carrots, onion, water, and garlic. Micro-cook, covered, on 100% power (HIGH) about 10 minutes or till vegetables are crisp-tender, stirring after 5 minutes. Stir in cabbage.

½	cup hot water
2½	teaspoons instant beef bouillon granules
1½	teaspoons caraway seed
2	tablespoons all-purpose flour
1	8-ounce carton plain yogurt *or* dairy sour cream

● Stir together water, bouillon granules, and caraway till granules are dissolved. Add to vegetable mixture. Micro-cook, covered, on 100% power (HIGH) 4½ minutes, stirring once.

Stir flour into yogurt or sour cream. Stir into vegetable mixture. Micro-cook, uncovered, on 100% power (HIGH) 2 minutes, stirring once. Stir again.

2	4-ounce packages thin-sliced hard salami

● Fold the salami into quarters, then arrange around outer edge of the casserole, pressing salami into vegetable mixture. Micro-cook, uncovered, on 100% power (HIGH) 2½ minutes. Spoon off fat. Serves 6.

Creamy Chicken and Rice

| 1 | 2½- to 3-pound broiler-fryer chicken, cut up |
| 1 | medium onion, cut into thin wedges |

● In a 12x7½x2-inch baking dish arrange chicken with meaty portions to outside of the dish. Add onion. Cover with vented clear plastic wrap. Micro-cook on 100% power (HIGH) 8 minutes. Remove chicken, then drain onions and return onions to the dish.

1½	cups quick-cooking rice
1	10¾-ounce can condensed cream of mushroom soup
1	cup water
2	tablespoons snipped parsley
2	tablespoons dry sherry
¼	cup toasted, sliced almonds
	Paprika

● Stir rice, soup, water, parsley, and sherry into the dish. Arrange chicken atop with meaty portions to outside of the dish. Cover with vented clear plastic wrap. Micro-cook on 100% power (HIGH) 8 to 10 minutes or till chicken is done, turning chicken over and rearranging once. Cover and let stand 5 minutes. Arrange chicken on a platter. Stir rice and spoon around chicken. Sprinkle almonds and paprika atop. Makes 4 servings.

Dress up Creamy Chicken and Rice with quick-as-a-wink toasted, sliced almonds. In a 1-cup measure micro-cook almonds, uncovered, on 100% power (HIGH) 3 to 4 minutes or till toasted, stirring every 30 seconds.

Quick Minestrone

| 3 | slices bacon, cut up |
| 1 | medium onion, chopped (½ cup) |

● In a 2-quart casserole micro-cook bacon, covered, on 100% power (HIGH) about 2½ minutes or till almost crisp, stirring once. Add onion. Micro-cook, covered, on 100% power (HIGH) 2 to 3 minutes or till onion is tender. Drain and remove from the casserole.

¼	cup chopped celery
¼	cup sliced carrots
2	8-ounce cans red kidney beans or pinto beans, drained
½	of a 15½-ounce jar spaghetti sauce
¼	cup small shell macaroni
1½	teaspoons instant beef bouillon granules
⅛	teaspoon minced dried garlic

● In same casserole combine celery, carrots, and 1 tablespoon *water*. Micro-cook, covered, on 100% power (HIGH) 2 to 3 minutes or till vegetables are crisp-tender. Stir in bacon mixture, beans, spaghetti sauce, macaroni, bouillon granules, garlic, 3 cups *water*, and ¼ teaspoon *pepper*. Micro-cook, covered, on 100% power (HIGH) 10 minutes, stirring once.

For a light but warming lunch on a blustery day, fix Quick Minestrone. The secret to its well-rounded flavor is half of a jar of spaghetti sauce.

¼	cup chopped zucchini
¼	cup grated Parmesan cheese
	Snipped parsley

● Stir in zucchini. Micro-cook, covered, on 100% power (HIGH) 5 to 8 minutes or till macaroni is tender. Ladle into soup bowls. Sprinkle each serving with Parmesan cheese and parsley. Serves 3.

Shortcut Gumbo

½ of a 10-ounce package
  frozen cut okra
1 14½-ounce can stewed
  tomatoes, cut up
1 6-ounce can spicy
  vegetable juice cocktail
1 tablespoon minced dried
  onion
2 teaspoons Worcestershire
  sauce
1½ teaspoons lemon juice
1 teaspoon instant chicken
  bouillon granules
½ teaspoon dried thyme,
  crushed
¼ teaspoon minced dried
  garlic
¼ teaspoon ground red
  pepper
¼ teaspoon ground allspice
1 bay leaf

● Thaw okra (see tip, page 17). In a 2-quart casserole combine okra, *undrained* tomatoes, vegetable juice cocktail, onion, Worcestershire sauce, lemon juice, bouillon granules, thyme, garlic, red pepper, and allspice. Add bay leaf.

Micro-cook, covered, on 100% power (HIGH) 6 minutes, stirring once.

Filé (pronounced fih-LAY) powder—powdered sassafras leaves—is a hallmark of many gumbos and other creole dishes. Creole cooks add this seasoning after removing a dish from the heat so the filé won't string.

½ of a 16-ounce package
  frozen and deveined
  shrimp
3 ounces fully cooked ham,
  cut into ½-inch cubes
  (⅔ cup)
2 teaspoons filé powder
  Hot cooked rice

● Stir in shrimp and ham. Micro-cook, covered, on 100% power (HIGH) 6 to 7 minutes or till shrimp turns pink, stirring twice. Remove bay leaf. Stir in filé powder. Spoon rice into soup plates. Ladle gumbo over rice. Serves 4.

No-Measure Beef Stew

1 pound beef stew meat, cut into ½-inch cubes
2 medium sweet potatoes, peeled and cut into 1-inch pieces
2 medium parsnips, peeled and cut into ½-inch pieces
1 medium onion, sliced and separated into rings
1 15-ounce can tomato-herb sauce

1 large green pepper, cut into thin strips

● In a 3-quart casserole combine beef, sweet potatoes, parsnips, and onion. Stir in tomato-herb sauce. Use tomato-herb sauce can to measure ½ can *water*. Stir into vegetable mixture. Micro-cook, covered, on 100% power (HIGH) about 7 minutes or till bubbly; stir. Reduce power to 50% (MEDIUM). Micro-cook, covered, 45 to 50 minutes more or till meat is tender, stirring twice.

● Stir in green pepper. Micro-cook, covered, on 50% power (MEDIUM) about 5 minutes more or till green pepper is crisp-tender. Skim off fat. Stir before serving. Makes 6 to 8 servings.

Shepherd's Pie

1 **pound bulk Italian sausage *or* bulk pork sausage** 1 **medium onion, chopped (½ cup)**	● Crumble sausage into a 2-quart casserole, then stir in onion. Micro-cook, covered, on 100% power (HIGH) 5 to 6 minutes or till sausage is no longer pink, stirring twice to break up sausage. Drain off fat. Remove from casserole.	For the shepherd on a tight schedule, our version calls for instant potato buds instead of regular mashed spuds. The result is a topper for this sausage-and-vegetable stew that's just as easy as it is tasty.
1⅓ **cups water** ⅓ **cup milk** 2 **tablespoons butter *or* margarine** ½ **teaspoon salt** 1⅓ **cups packaged instant mashed potato buds** 1 **teaspoon dried parsley flakes**	● Meanwhile, in a 4-cup measure stir together water, milk, butter or margarine, and salt. Micro-cook, uncovered, on 100% power (HIGH) 4 to 7 minutes or till boiling. Stir in potato buds and parsley flakes.	
1 **10-ounce package frozen peas and carrots** 2 **tablespoons water** 1 **10¾-ounce can condensed tomato soup** 1 **cup shredded cheddar cheese (4 ounces)**	● In the 2-quart casserole micro-cook peas and carrots and water, covered, on 100% power (HIGH) 5 to 6 minutes or till crisp-tender. Drain. Stir in sausage mixture and soup. Spoon mounds of potato mixture over sausage and vegetable mixture. Micro-cook, uncovered, on 100% power (HIGH) 6 to 7 minutes or till heated through, rotating the dish once. Top with cheese. Micro-cook, uncovered, on 100% power (HIGH) 2 to 3 minutes or till cheese is melted, rotating the casserole once. Makes 4 servings.	

Freezer Beef Base

2 pounds beef round steak, cut into ½-inch cubes

● In a 2-quart casserole micro-cook beef, covered, on 100% power (HIGH) 8 to 10 minutes or till done, stirring twice. Remove beef, reserving juices in the dish.

1 medium onion, chopped (½ cup)
1 stalk celery, thinly sliced (½ cup)
1 tablespoon instant beef bouillon granules
1 tablespoon Worcestershire sauce

● Stir onion, celery, bouillon granules, and Worcestershire sauce into reserved juices. Micro-cook, covered, on 100% power (HIGH) 6 to 7 minutes or till vegetables are crisp-tender. Stir in beef. Spoon *half* of the beef mixture into each of 2 moisture- and vaporproof containers. Seal, label, and freeze. Makes about 4 cups.

Ever find a UFO—unidentified frozen object—in your freezer? Eliminate the confusion by labeling each item with its contents and the date you freeze it (or add the date you must use the food by). The bases in this chapter will freeze well for two to four months.

Freezer Chicken Base

3 pounds chicken drumsticks *or* thighs, skinned
3 stalks celery, thinly sliced (1½ cups)
2 carrots, shredded (1 cup)
3 green onions, sliced (¼ cup)
¼ cup water
1 tablespoon instant chicken bouillon granules
½ teaspoon dried thyme, crushed
¼ teaspoon pepper

● In a 3-quart casserole combine chicken, celery, carrots, onions, water, bouillon granules, thyme, and pepper. Micro-cook, covered, on 100% power (HIGH) 20 to 30 minutes or till chicken is done and vegetables are tender, stirring and rearranging chicken twice. Cool till easy to handle.

It would be a crime to waste all the good flavor in the cooking juices (stock). Store the stock to use in soups or for cooking rice. It will keep three or four days in the refrigerator or six months in the freezer. If you frequently use stock in small amounts, freeze it in ice cube trays. When frozen, place the cubes in a plastic bag and return them to the freezer.

● Drain, reserving juices for another use. Remove chicken from bones, then cube chicken. Spoon half of the chicken-and-vegetable mixture into each of 2 moisture- and vaporproof containers. Seal, label, and freeze. Makes 3¾ cups.

Freezer Meatball Base

2 slightly beaten eggs
⅓ cup milk
2 cups soft bread crumbs (2⅔ slices)
1 medium onion, chopped (½ cup)
½ teaspoon salt
½ teaspoon dried thyme, crushed
1 pound ground beef
1 pound ground pork

● In a large bowl combine eggs and milk. Stir in bread crumbs, onion, salt, and thyme. Add meat, then mix well. Shape meat mixture into 48 meatballs.

In a 9-inch pie plate arrange 16 meatballs in a circle. Micro-cook meatballs, uncovered, on 100% power (HIGH) about 4 minutes or till no longer pink, turning meatballs over and rearranging once. Remove the meatballs to paper towels. Repeat until all meatballs are cooked.

● Place meatballs on a baking pan, then place in freezer till just frozen. Using 16 meatballs per package, wrap in 3 moisture- and vaporproof containers. Seal, label, and freeze. Makes 48.

Shaping meatballs is a cinch if you keep this tip in mind. Form the meat mixture into a roll 1½ inches in diameter. Then, cut 1½-inch slices and shape them into balls.

Freezer Wrap-Ups

You can't tell a book by its cover. When it comes to frozen foods, however, the cover packaging tells you a lot about the quality of what's inside. Leaky cover packaging lets moisture escape and that leads to freezer burn—a grayish white discoloring of the food.

To avoid freezer burn, package foods in moisture- and vaporproof wrap or containers. That means the wrap-up must keep moisture in and air out. The wrapping also should be odorless, tasteless, and sturdy. Your best bets are freezer paper, heavy foil, freezer bags, rigid plastic containers, or glass freezer jars.

Chicken Enchiladas

1	**package Freezer Chicken Base (see recipe, page 42)**
1	**cup shredded American cheese (4 ounces)**
¼	**cup taco sauce**
1	**tablespoon diced green chili peppers**

● In a 2-quart casserole micro-cook chicken base, covered, on 50% power (MEDIUM) about 5 minutes or till thawed, stirring once to break up base. Stir in cheese, taco sauce, and green chili peppers.

Stoke the fire of your enchiladas—or calm it down. You decide by choosing a mild or hot taco sauce.

6	**6-inch corn tortillas**
¾	**cup taco sauce**
½	**cup shredded American cheese (2 ounces)**
	Shredded lettuce (optional)
1	**medium tomato, chopped (optional)**
½	**cup dairy sour cream (optional)**
¼	**cup sliced pitted ripe olives (optional)**

● Spoon about ⅓ *cup* chicken mixture into center of each tortilla. Roll up and place seam side down in a 12x7½x2-inch baking dish. Spoon taco sauce atop. Cover with vented clear plastic wrap. Micro-cook on 100% power (HIGH) 5 to 8 minutes or till heated through, rotating the dish a half-turn every 3 minutes. Sprinkle with cheese. Micro-cook, covered, on 100% power (HIGH) about 1 minute or till cheese is melted. If desired, top with lettuce, tomato, sour cream, and olives. Makes 3 servings.

Freezer Lowdown

Once you discover the variety of one-dish meals that start with our freezer bases, you'll want to make the recipes often. To ensure top-notch meals every time, follow these easy tips when freezing the bases.

● Start with first-rate ingredients. Quality and flavor don't improve with freezing.

● Be extra careful about sanitary conditions. Freezer temperatures of 0° F or below only stop the growth of bacteria; they don't kill bacteria.

● Use a freezer thermometer to make sure the freezer temperature is 0° F or below.

● It's better to slightly undercook than overcook the bases. They'll get more cooking later.

● After cooking, chill the bases quickly by placing the containers in ice water to cool to room temperature. Otherwise, the hot bases will raise the temperature in your freezer. Also, to maintain a constant temperature, avoid adding too much to the freezer at one time.

Curried Chicken and Rice

1	package Freezer Chicken Base (see recipe, page 42)

● In a 2-quart casserole micro-cook chicken base, covered, on 50% power (MEDIUM) about 5 minutes or till thawed, stirring once to break up base.

1	14½-ounce can tomatoes, cut up
⅔	cup quick-cooking rice
½	of a small green pepper, finely chopped (¼ cup)
2	tablespoons hot water
2 to 3	teaspooons curry powder
½	cup salted peanuts
½	cup raisins
2	tablespoons snipped parsley (optional)

● Stir in *undrained* tomatoes, *uncooked* rice, green pepper, water, and curry powder. Micro-cook, covered, on 100% power (HIGH) 8 to 10 minutes or till rice is tender, stirring twice. Stir in peanuts and raisins. Top with parsley, if desired. Makes 4 servings.

Curry powder is really a convenience food in disguise. Sometimes 16 or more spices go into curry powder. Each blend differs slightly, but almost always curry includes cumin, coriander, fenugreek, turmeric, and red pepper. In India, where curry cookery is an art, the blend of spices and, consequently, the hotness of the foods vary from region to region.

Vegetable Beef Soup

1	package Freezer Beef Base (see recipe, page 42)

● In a 2-quart casserole micro-cook base, covered, on 50% power (MEDIUM) about 8 minutes or till thawed, stirring once to break up base.

1	14½-ounce can tomatoes, cut up
1¾	cups beef broth
½	of a 10-ounce package (1 cup) frozen lima beans
2	carrots, thinly sliced
1	tablespoon minced dried onion
½	teaspoon dried thyme, crushed

● Stir in *undrained* tomatoes, broth, lima beans, carrots, onion, thyme, and ⅛ teaspoon *pepper*. Micro-cook, covered, on 100% power (HIGH) 12 to 15 minutes or till boiling, stirring once. Reduce power to 70% (MEDIUM-HIGH). Micro-cook, covered, about 30 minutes or till meat and vegetables are tender, stirring twice. Makes 4 servings.

Everybody has certain "comfort" foods that conjure up feelings of warmth and security. We think our version of Vegetable Beef Soup qualifies. Serve it with crackers or a roll for an especially satisfying meal that's sure to earn a special place in your heart.

Vegetable Beef Soup

Burgundy Beef and Asparagus
(see recipe, page 48)

Beef and Cabbage
(see recipe, page 49)

Burgundy Beef and Asparagus

Pictured on page 47.

1 package Freezer Beef Base (see recipe, page 42) 1 pound fresh asparagus, cut into 1-inch pieces, *or* one 10-ounce package frozen cut asparagus	● In a 2-quart casserole micro-cook beef base, covered, on 50% power (MEDIUM) about 8 minutes or till thawed, stirring once to break up base. Thaw asparagus (see tip, page 17), if frozen; set asparagus aside.	**Raid the cupboard and the freezer for this spirited entrée. If you use frozen cut asparagus, all of the ingredients are easy to keep on hand for drop-in dinner guests.**
¾ cup water ½ cup burgundy 1 4½-ounce jar whole mushrooms 1 ¾-ounce envelope mushroom gravy mix	● Stir water and burgundy into beef base. Micro-cook, covered, on 100% power (HIGH) about 7 minutes or till boiling. Reduce power to 70% (MEDIUM-HIGH). Micro-cook, covered, about 30 minutes or till meat is tender, stirring once. Stir in asparagus, *undrained* mushrooms, and gravy mix. Micro-cook, covered, on 100% power (HIGH) 4 to 6 minutes or till asparagus is crisp-tender.	
2 tablespoons cold water 4 teaspoons all-purpose flour Hot cooked noodles *or* rice	● Stir together water and flour. Stir into beef mixture. Micro-cook, uncovered, on 100% power (HIGH) 1 to 2 minutes or till thickened and bubbly, stirring every minute. Serve atop noodles or rice. Makes 4 servings.	

Beef and Cabbage

Pictured on page 47.

The zing in this robust one-dish meal comes from pepperoni and an apple-cider-and-mustard sauce.

1 package Freezer Beef Base (see recipe, page 42) 1¼ cups apple cider *or* juice 4 cups shredded cabbage	● In a 2-quart casserole micro-cook base and apple cider or juice, covered, on 50% power (MEDIUM) about 8 minutes or till base is thawed, stirring once to break up base. Micro-cook, covered, on 100% power (HIGH) 3 to 5 minutes or till boiling. Reduce power to 70% (MEDIUM-HIGH). Micro-cook, covered, about 30 minutes or till base is tender, stirring once. Stir in cabbage. Micro-cook, covered, on 100% power 5 to 6 minutes or till cabbage is crisp-tender.
2 tablespoons apple cider *or* juice 1 tablespoon Dijon-style mustard 2 teaspoons cornstarch ⅓ cup coarsely chopped pepperoni	● In a 2-cup measure combine apple cider or juice, mustard, and cornstarch. Stir apple juice mixture and pepperoni into beef mixture. Micro-cook, uncovered, on 100% power (HIGH) 1 to 2 minutes or till thickened and bubbly, stirring once. Makes 4 servings.

Finishing Touches

Jazz up a one-dish meal with any of these garnishes.
● The easiest dress-up may be an ingredient in the dish itself. Save some cooked carrot or olive slices, mushrooms, toasted nuts, or snipped parsley to sprinkle over your one-dish meal just before serving. Or, slice an extra tomato or green pepper to arrange atop the dish during the last few minutes of cooking.
● Check your refrigerator or kitchen shelves—many ingredients you have on hand can be garnishes. Use lemon or avocado slices to perk up seafood dishes, use pineapple or poached apple slices to complement ham and pork dishes, or use croutons or canned french-fried onions to spruce up a casserole.
● Make an easy casserole topper from crushed crackers, crushed cereal, or stuffing mix. Just stir the crumbs into some melted butter and sprinkle around the outer edge of the casserole (see Salmon-Noodle Bake, page 27).

Spaghetti Squash and Meatballs

It's amazing! Spaghetti squash makes great mock pasta with about one-eighth the calories of the real thing.

1 2- to 3-pound spaghetti squash, halved lengthwise 2 tablespoons water	● Remove seeds from squash. Place squash halves, cut side down, in a 12x7½x2-inch baking dish. Sprinkle with water, then cover with vented clear plastic wrap. Micro-cook on 100% power (HIGH) 14 to 18 minutes or till pulp can be pierced with a fork, rotating the dish twice. Let stand, covered, 10 minutes.
1 medium green pepper, chopped (¾ cup) 1 medium onion, chopped (½ cup) 2 tablespoons water	● Meanwhile, in a 2-quart casserole micro-cook pepper, onion, and water, covered, on 100% power (HIGH) 2 to 3 minutes or till onion is tender.
1 15½-ounce jar extra-thick spaghetti sauce 1 package Freezer Meatball Base (see recipe, page 43) Grated Parmesan cheese	● Stir in spaghetti sauce and frozen meatballs. Micro-cook, covered, on 100% power (HIGH) 7 to 9 minutes or till heated through, stirring twice. Use a fork to shred and separate squash pulp into strands. Pile onto a serving platter. Serve meatball mixture over squash. Pass Parmesan cheese. Makes 4 servings.

Meatballs with French Onion Sauce

1 **medium onion, sliced** 2 **tablespoons butter** *or* **margarine** 2 **tablespoons cornstarch** 2 **tablespoons cold water** 1 **10½-ounce can condensed beef broth** ¼ **teaspoon Worcestershire sauce** 1 **package Freezer Meatball Base (see recipe, page 43)** 2 **tablespoons snipped parsley**	● In a 2-quart casserole micro-cook onion and butter or margarine, covered, on 100% power (HIGH) 4 to 5 minutes or till onion is tender, stirring once. Mix cornstarch and water, then stir into onion mixture. Stir in broth and Worcestershire sauce. Stir in frozen meatballs. Micro-cook, uncovered, on 100% power (HIGH) 7 to 9 minutes or till meatballs are heated through, stirring every 2 minutes. Stir in parsley. Micro-cook, uncovered, on 100% power (HIGH) 1 minute more.
4 **slices French bread, bias-sliced and toasted** 4 **slices Swiss cheese**	● Place bread slices on 4 individual plates, then place a cheese slice atop bread. Spoon meatball mixture atop. Makes 4 servings.

Start with the French bread, top it with Swiss cheese, and finish with a sauce full of meatballs and onions. You'll end up with upside-down French onion soup.

Sauerbraten Meatballs

1 **cup apple juice** 1 **8-ounce can tomato sauce** 2 **tablespoons vinegar** 1 **teaspoon prepared mustard** **Dash pepper** 1 **package Freezer Meatball Base (see recipe, page 43)**	● For sauce, in a 2-quart casserole stir together apple juice, tomato sauce, vinegar, mustard, and pepper. Stir in frozen meatballs. Micro-cook, covered, on 100% power (HIGH) 5 to 7 minutes or till meatballs are heated through, stirring twice.
6 **gingersnaps, crushed** **Hot cooked spaetzle** *or* **noodles** 2 **tablespoons snipped parsley (optional)**	● Stir gingersnaps into sauce. Micro-cook, uncovered, on 100% power (HIGH) about 3 minutes or till thickened and bubbly, stirring every minute. Serve over spaetzle or noodles. Sprinkle with parsley, if desired. Makes 4 servings.

Just as we'd do with an authentic sauerbraten, we thickened our sweet-and-sour sauce with crushed gingersnaps.

Sausage and Apple Pastitsio

1 cup elbow macaroni ¾ pound bulk pork sausage 1 medium onion, chopped (½ cup)	● Cook macaroni according to package directions. Drain and set aside. Meanwhile, crumble sausage into an 8x8x2-inch baking dish, then stir in onion. Cover with vented clear plastic wrap. Micro-cook on 100% power (HIGH) 4 to 6 minutes or till sausage is no longer pink and onion is tender, stirring once to break up sausage. Drain.
1 medium cooking apple, peeled, cored, and chopped (1 cup) 1 8-ounce can tomato sauce ½ cup raisins 2 tablespoons grated Parmesan cheese ¼ teaspoon ground cinnamon	● Stir in apple, tomato sauce, raisins, cheese, and cinnamon. Stir in macaroni. Spread mixture evenly in the dish.
2 tablespoons butter *or* margarine 2 tablespoons cornstarch ¼ teaspoon salt 1 cup milk 2 slightly beaten eggs 2 tablespoons grated Parmesan cheese	● In a 4-cup measure micro-cook butter or margarine, uncovered, on 100% power (HIGH) 40 to 50 seconds or till melted. Stir in cornstarch and salt. Stir in milk. Micro-cook, uncovered, on 100% power (HIGH) 2 to 4 minutes or till thickened and bubbly, stirring every minute. Gradually stir ½ cup of the hot mixture into eggs. Return all to the 4-cup measure. Stir in cheese. Set aside.
Ground cinnamon	● Micro-cook sausage mixture, uncovered, on 100% power (HIGH) 6 to 8 minutes or till heated through, stirring once. Immediately pour egg mixture atop hot sausage mixture. Sprinkle with cinnamon. Micro-cook, uncovered, on 100% power (HIGH) 5 to 8 minutes or till topping is just set, rotating the dish a quarter-turn 3 times. Let stand, uncovered, 10 minutes. Serves 6.

To make sure the custard topping gets done in the center as well as around the edges, pour the egg mixture over the sausage mixture as soon as it comes piping hot out of the microwave oven.

Shrimp with Gruyère Sauce

1½ **pounds fresh *or* frozen shrimp in shells**	● To thaw shrimp, in a 2-quart casserole micro-cook, uncovered, on 50% power (MEDIUM) about 5 minutes or till nearly thawed, stirring once. Let stand, uncovered, about 6 minutes or till completely thawed. Shell and devein shrimp, then halve lengthwise.
1 **10-ounce package frozen cut asparagus** 2 **tablespoons water**	● Meanwhile, thaw asparagus (see tip, page 17). In the 2-quart casserole micro-cook shrimp, asparagus, and water, covered, on 100% power (HIGH) 6 to 8 minutes or till shrimp turn pink and asparagus is crisp-tender. Drain and remove from casserole. Set aside.
2 **tablespoons butter *or* margarine** 2 **tablespoons all-purpose flour** 1 **cup light cream *or* milk** 1 **teaspoon Dijon-style mustard**	● For sauce, in the casserole micro-cook butter or margarine, uncovered, on 100% power (HIGH) 40 to 50 seconds or till melted. Stir in flour. Stir in cream or milk and mustard all at once. Micro-cook, uncovered, on 100% power (HIGH) 2 to 3 minutes or till thickened and bubbly, stirring every minute.
½ **cup shredded Gruyère cheese (2 ounces)** 1 **tablespoon lemon juice** **Hot cooked wild rice *or* long grain rice** **Paprika (optional)**	● Stir in cheese and lemon juice till cheese is melted. Stir shrimp and asparagus into sauce. Micro-cook, uncovered, on 100% power (HIGH) about 1 minute or till heated through. Serve over rice. Sprinkle paprika atop, if desired. Makes 4 servings.

Sweet and nutlike—that's the flavor of Gruyère cheese. And it's what makes this shrimp and asparagus dish extra-elegant.

Broccoli and Veal Bundles

1 **pound boneless veal leg round steak, cut ½ inch thick** **Salt**	● Cut veal into 4 pieces. Place 1 piece of veal between 2 pieces of clear plastic wrap. Working from center to edges, pound lightly with flat side of a meat mallet, forming a rectangle about ⅛ inch thick. Remove clear plastic wrap. Sprinkle veal with salt. Repeat with remaining veal.
1 **10-ounce package frozen chopped broccoli** 1 **carrot, shredded (½ cup)** 2 **tablespoons sliced green onion** ¼ **teaspoon pepper** ½ **cup shredded Swiss cheese (2 ounces)**	● Thaw broccoli (see tip, page 17). Drain. In a small bowl combine broccoli, carrot, onion, and pepper. Spread *one-fourth* of the broccoli mixture to within ½ inch of the edge of *each* piece of meat. Sprinkle cheese atop. Fold in sides and ends. Use wooden toothpicks to secure bundles, if necessary.
1 **tablespoon butter *or* margarine**	● In an 8x8x2-inch baking dish micro-cook butter, uncovered, on 100% power (HIGH) 30 to 40 seconds or till melted. Arrange veal rolls in baking dish, then brush with butter. Micro-cook, uncovered, on 100% power (HIGH) 4 minutes, rearranging rolls once. Cover with vented clear plastic wrap. Micro-cook on 50% power (MEDIUM) 4 to 6 minutes or till meat is done, rearranging rolls once. Drain off juices, reserving ⅓ cup. Cover meat with foil to keep warm.
2 **tablespoons cold water** 2 **teaspoons cornstarch** 1 **tablespoon dry sherry** ½ **teaspoon instant beef bouillon granules** ¼ **teaspoon dried thyme, crushed** **Few drops Kitchen Bouquet (optional)** 2 **tablespoons snipped parsley**	● For sauce, strain juices. If necessary, add water to make ⅓ cup. In a 2-cup measure stir together water and cornstarch. Stir in reserved juices, sherry, bouillon granules, thyme, and, if desired, Kitchen Bouquet. Micro-cook, uncovered, on 100% power (HIGH) 1 to 2 minutes or till thickened and bubbly, stirring every 30 seconds. Transfer rolls to a platter, then pour sauce atop. Sprinkle with parsley. Makes 4 servings.

In Old Testament times, veal, otherwise known as the fatted calf, was food fit for a feast. Next time you have reason to celebrate, or even if you don't, try Broccoli-Veal Roll with its colorful vegetable stuffing and rich sauce.

To avoid tearing the tender veal, use the flat side of a meat mallet to pound each piece into a rectangle about ⅛ inch thick.

To form bundles, fold sides and ends of the veal over the broccoli mixture. Secure with wooden toothpicks, if necessary.

Pork Chops and Rice Dijon

1 10-ounce package frozen peas and carrots 1 tablespoon cooking oil 4 pork chops, cut ½ inch thick and trimmed of separable fat	● Thaw peas and carrots (see tip, page 17). Set aside. Preheat a 10-inch microwave browning dish on 100% power (HIGH) 5 minutes. Add cooking oil, then swirl to coat dish. Add pork chops. Micro-cook, uncovered, on 100% power (HIGH) 4 minutes, turning chops after 2 minutes. Remove chops.
1 10¾-ounce can condensed cream of celery soup ½ cup dry white wine 1 to 2 tablespoons Dijon-style mustard ¾ cup quick-cooking rice 1 4-ounce can mushroom stems and pieces, drained	● Meanwhile, in a medium mixing bowl stir together soup, wine, and mustard. Reserve ½ cup of soup mixture. Stir peas and carrots, *uncooked* rice, and mushrooms into remaining soup mixture.
Snipped parsley (optional)	● Transfer rice mixture to the browning dish. Arrange chops atop with meatiest portions to outside of the dish. Spoon reserved soup mixture over chops. Micro-cook, covered, on 70% power (MEDIUM-HIGH) about 20 minutes or till pork is no longer pink near the bone, rotating the dish a half-turn every 5 minutes. Transfer pork to a serving platter. Stir rice mixture and spoon onto the platter. Sprinkle parsley atop, if desired. Makes 4 servings.

French cooks take mustard seriously. That's why in Dijon, France, they tested and tinkered with dry mustard, herbs, spices, and white wine until they came up with the tart yet pleasing flavor of their creamy mustard. But you don't have to go to France for good mustard. Your local grocery store carries Dijon-style mustard made in America.

Christmas Eve Dinner For Four

When the occasion calls for something special, try this light and delicious menu that's as festive as can be yet quick as a wink. Because you prepare most of it in the microwave oven, you can relax and enjoy the good company (see recipes, pages 58-59).

MENU
Tarragon Spinach Salad
Chicken à l'Orange
Rolls with whipped butter
Dutch Apple Cake
White Wine Spritzers

MENU COUNTDOWN
Several Hours Ahead:
Prepare salad dressing for Tarragon Spinach Salad; chill. Wash salad ingredients; chill.

2 Hours Ahead:
Make Dutch Apple Cake.
1 Hour Ahead:
Prepare Chicken à l'Orange. Finish assembling Tarragon Spinach Salad.
At Serving Time:
Prepare White Wine Spritzers.

White Wine Spritzers

Pictured on pages 56–57.

1 **750-milliliter bottle dry white wine, chilled** 2 **cups carbonated water, lemon-lime carbonated beverage,** *or* **ginger ale, chilled** **Carambola, sliced and seeds removed (optional)**	● Just before serving, fill each of 4 glasses two-thirds full of wine. Add enough carbonated water, lemon-lime carbonated beverage, or ginger ale to almost fill glass. Stir gently. Garnish with a slice of carambola on edge of the glass, if desired. Makes 4 servings.

These spritzers feature a wonderfully special garnish—carambola, also called star fruit. The flesh is juicy and may be sweet or sour depending on the variety. No need to peel it. The skin is edible.

Chicken à l'Orange

Pictured on page 56.

½ **teaspoon finely shredded orange peel** ¾ **cup orange juice** 1 **tablespoon soy sauce** 1½ **teaspoons cornstarch** ¼ **teaspoon garlic powder**	● For sauce, in a 2-cup measure stir together orange peel, orange juice, soy sauce, cornstarch, and garlic. Micro-cook, uncovered, on 100% power (HIGH) 2 to 4 minutes or till thickened and bubbly, stirring every minute; set aside.
2 **whole large chicken breasts (2 pounds total), skinned, boned, and halved lengthwise**	● Arrange chicken in a 10x6x2-inch baking dish with meatiest portions to outside of the dish. Cover with vented clear plastic wrap. Micro-cook on 100% power (HIGH) 3 to 4 minutes or till just done, turning chicken once. Remove chicken and drain dish.
2 **medium carrots, cut into julienne strips (1 cup)** 2 **tablespoons water** 1 **6-ounce package frozen pea pods**	● Place carrots and water in the baking dish. Cover with vented clear plastic wrap. Micro-cook on 100% power (HIGH) about 2 mintues or till almost tender. Add pea pods. Micro-cook on 100% power (HIGH) 2 to 3 minutes or till pea pods are crisp-tender. Drain.
Orange slices (optional)	● Place chicken atop vegetables. Pour sauce atop. Cover with vented clear plastic wrap. Micro-cook on 100% power (HIGH) 30 to 60 seconds or till heated through. Garnish with orange slices, if desired. Makes 4 servings.

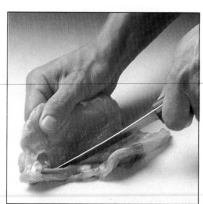

Save money by boning the chicken breasts yourself. To bone, place the chicken bone side down. Using a sharp knife, cut the meat away from the bone, working from breastbone to the outside. Repeat on other side of breast.

Tarragon Spinach Salad

Pictured on page 56.

2 tablespoons white wine vinegar 1 tablespoon salad oil 1½ teaspoons snipped fresh tarragon *or* ½ teaspoon dried tarragon, crushed 1 teaspoon sugar ⅛ teaspoon dry mustard	● For dressing, in a screw-top jar combine vinegar, oil, tarragon, sugar, dry mustard, 1 tablespoon *water,* and ⅛ teaspoon *salt.* Cover and shake well. (To store dressing, chill in the refrigerator.)
3 cups torn fresh spinach ¾ cup sliced fresh mushrooms 1 avocado, halved, pitted, peeled, and sliced 1 small onion, sliced and separated into rings	● In a large bowl combine spinach, mushrooms, avocado, and onion. Shake dressing well and pour over salad. Toss lightly to coat. Makes 4 servings.

This versatile vinaigrette dressing complements just about any fresh-vegetable combination.

Dutch Apple Cake

Pictured on page 57.

¼ cup chopped walnuts 1 cup all-purpose flour 1 cup whole wheat flour 1 teaspoon baking powder 1 teaspoon ground cinnamon ½ teaspoon baking soda 2 eggs 1 teaspoon vanilla	● Lightly grease a 10-inch microwave fluted tube pan. Sprinkle walnuts on bottom and sides of the pan. In a large mixing bowl stir together flours, baking powder, cinnamon, baking soda, and ½ teaspoon *salt.* Set aside. In a large mixer bowl combine eggs and vanilla, then beat on high speed of an electric mixer for 2 minutes or till light.
1 cup cooking oil 1 cup packed brown sugar ½ cup sugar 3 medium apples, peeled, cored, and chopped ¾ cup chopped walnuts	● Gradually add oil, beating for 2 minutes or till thick. Gradually beat in sugars. Add dry ingredients alternately with apples and walnuts, beating well on low speed after each addition. Beat at medium speed for 3 minutes. Turn batter into the tube pan.
Cream Cheese Icing (see recipe, at right)	● Micro-cook, uncovered, on 50% power (MEDIUM) 14 to 16 minutes, rotating the pan a quarter-turn every 4 minutes. Rotate the pan again. Micro-cook, uncovered, on 100% power (HIGH) about 1½ minutes or till surface appears nearly dry, rotating a half-turn once. Cool 10 minutes. Invert cake onto a serving plate. Remove pan and cool. Drizzle cake with icing. Serves 10 to 12.

Here's how to make ultra-creamy Cream Cheese Icing: In a small mixer bowl beat together one 3-ounce package softened *cream cheese* and 1 cup sifted *powdered sugar* till fluffy. Beat in ¼ teaspoon *vanilla.* If necessary, beat in enough *milk* (about 1 teaspoon) to make a frosting of spreading consistency. Drizzle over top of cooled cake. If desired, garnish with apple slices, chopped walnuts, and cranberries.

Bouillabaisse

10 ounces fresh *or* frozen cod
  or haddock fillets
8 ounces frozen lobster-tail
1 pound fresh *or* frozen
  shrimp in shells

● In a 3-quart casserole micro-cook fish, if frozen, and lobster, uncovered, on 30% power (MEDIUM-LOW) 4 minutes. Add shrimp, if frozen. Micro-cook, uncovered, on 30% power (MEDIUM-LOW) 11 to 14 minutes or till nearly thawed, separating and rearranging pieces every 4 minutes. Let stand about 5 minutes or till thawed. Shell and devein shrimp. Cut up lobster as shown at right. Cut fish into 1-inch pieces. Set seafood aside.

Use kitchen shears to cut lengthwise through the hard lobster shell. Turn lobster-tail over and cut through underside shell and meat. Cut each halved lobster-tail crosswise through shell and meat three or four times to make six or eight pieces total.

3 medium onions, chopped
2 tablespoons olive oil *or*
  cooking oil
2 cloves garlic, minced
1 14½-ounce can tomatoes,
  cut up
1½ cups water
¼ cup snipped parsley
1 teaspoon salt
½ teaspoon finely shredded
  orange peel
½ teaspoon dried thyme,
  crushed
¼ teaspoon thread saffron,
  crushed
¼ teaspoon dried rosemary,
  crushed
1 pound clams in shells,
  rinsed

● In the 3-quart casserole micro-cook onions, oil, and garlic, covered, on 100% power (HIGH) 5 minutes, stirring once. Stir in next 8 ingredients and ¼ teaspoon *pepper*. Micro-cook, uncovered, on 100% power (HIGH) 5 to 6 minutes or till bubbly around edges, stirring once. Stir in fish, lobster, shrimp, and clams. Micro-cook, covered, on 100% power (HIGH) 10 to 12 minutes or till fish flakes easily when tested with a fork, stirring 3 times. Serves 4 to 6.

Beef Florentine

1	10-ounce package frozen chopped spinach	● Thaw spinach (see tip, page 17). Drain well, then set aside.
2	medium potatoes, peeled and cut into 1-inch pieces	In a medium bowl micro-cook potatoes and water, covered, on 100% power (HIGH) 7 to 9 minutes or till tender. Drain. Add butter or margarine, then cover and set aside.
¼	cup water	
1	tablespoon butter *or* margarine	

1	pound lean ground beef	● Crumble beef into a 1½-quart casserole, then stir in onion. Micro-cook, covered, on 100% power (HIGH) about 5 minutes or till beef is done, stirring once to break up meat. Drain off fat, then stir in cream cheese till softened.
1	medium onion, chopped (½ cup)	
1	3-ounce package cream cheese, cut up	

1	slightly beaten egg	● Stir in egg, bread crumbs, milk, salt, rosemary or marjoram, and pepper. Add spinach and mushrooms, then mix well. Micro-cook, uncovered, on 70% power (MEDIUM-HIGH) 6 to 8 minutes or till heated through, stirring twice.
½	cup soft bread crumbs	
½	cup milk	
½	teaspoon salt	
½	teaspoon dried rosemary *or* marjoram, crushed	
¼	teaspoon pepper	
1	2½-ounce jar sliced mushrooms, drained	

1	egg	● Meanwhile, mash hot potatoes. Beat in egg, parsley flakes, salt, and pepper. Beat in enough milk to make fluffy. Spoon mixture around edge.
1	teaspoon dried parsley flakes	Micro-cook, uncovered, on 70% power (MEDIUM-HIGH) 3 to 4 minutes or till potatoes are set, rotating the dish a half-turn once. Sprinkle with paprika, if desired. Makes 4 servings.
¼	teaspoon salt	
	Dash pepper	
1	to 2 tablespoons milk Paprika (optional)	

Make Beef Florentine as pleasing to the eye as it is to the palate. Use a pastry bag and a large tip to pipe the mashed potatoes around the outside edge of this hearty casserole. Beautiful!

Ham and Eggwiches

Pictured on pages 64–65.

6 beaten eggs
⅓ cup milk
2 tablespoons grated
   Parmesan cheese
1 tablespoon snipped
   parsley *or* 1 teaspoon
   dried parsley flakes
½ teaspoon onion powder
⅛ teaspoon pepper
1 6¾-ounce can chunk-style
   ham, drained and flaked
½ cup shredded American
   cheese (2 ounces)

● In a 1½-quart casserole combine eggs, milk, Parmesan cheese, parsley, onion powder, and pepper. Stir in ham. Micro-cook, uncovered, on 100% power (HIGH) 3 to 4 minutes or till almost set, pushing cooked portion to center several times. Stir in American cheese. Micro-cook, uncovered, on 100% power (HIGH) 1 to 2 minutes or till cheese is melted and eggs are set, but moist.

Wake up to sunshine with these get-your-day-going meal-in-one sandwiches. In less than 20 minutes you can have them on the table. They're real eye-openers.

3 English muffins, split and
   toasted
1 medium tomato, chopped
   (½ cup) (optional)
   Alfalfa sprouts (optional)
   Parsley (optional)

● Place 2 muffin halves on each of 3 individual plates. Top with egg mixture; tomato, if desired; and alfalfa sprouts, if desired. Garnish with parsley, if desired. Makes 3 servings.

Eggs That Excel

Nothing spoils a great recipe like tough eggs. To keep yours moist and tender when cooking recipes such as Ham and Eggwiches in the microwave oven, thoroughly beat the egg yolk and white together. Otherwise, the yolk (which has a high fat content and attracts micro-waves) will cook faster and become tough before the white is done. Another tip: As you cook an egg mixture, push the cooked portions to the center several times. That way, you avoid an undercooked center and over-cooked edges.

Knackwurst In Beer

1 cup beer
1 tablespoon brown sugar
1 tablespoon soy sauce
1½ teaspoons prepared mustard
½ teaspoon chili powder
1 clove garlic, minced
Few dashes bottled hot pepper sauce
4 5-inch links fully cooked knackwurst *or* smoked bratwurst

● For marinade, in a 2-cup measure combine beer, brown sugar, soy sauce, mustard, chili powder, garlic, and hot pepper sauce.

Cut deep diagonal slits 1 inch apart in each sausage link, cutting to but not through the opposite side. Place sausages in a shallow 8x8x2-inch baking dish. Pour marinade over sausage links. Cover and refrigerate several hours or overnight, spooning marinade over sausage occasionally.

The marinade has a real kick. That's why you cut deep slits in the knackwurst—to let all that good flavor seep into the sausage.

4 individual French rolls
1 8-ounce can sauerkraut, drained
½ cup shredded carrot

● Cut rolls in half lengthwise, then hollow out rolls, leaving a ¼-inch shell. (Save excess bread for another use.) Set aside. Remove sausages from marinade. Stir sauerkraut and carrot into marinade. Return sausages to baking dish. Micro-cook, uncovered, on 100% power (HIGH) 8 to 10 minutes or till heated through. Use a slotted spoon to fill each roll with some of the sauerkraut mixture, then top with a sausage and the roll top. Makes 4 servings.

Fiesta Pitas

Pictured on pages 64–65.

1 small *or* ½ of a medium avocado, pitted, peeled, and chopped
1 small tomato, seeded and chopped
2 tablespoons taco sauce
1 tablespoon sliced green onion

● For avocado salsa, in a small bowl stir together avocado, tomato, taco sauce, onion, and ⅛ teaspoon *salt*. Cover and chill till ready to use.

Break out of the same-old-sandwich rut. Try this snazzy rendition of the all-American hamburger hit. The spicy burger comes in a pita, and an avocado and tomato salsa adds to its fiesta flair.

1 beaten egg
2 tablespoons taco sauce
2 tablespoons regular rolled oats
2 tablespoons diced green chili peppers
1 teaspoon chili powder
½ teaspoon salt
¾ pound ground beef

● In a medium mixing bowl stir together egg and taco sauce. Stir in oats, chili peppers, chili powder, and salt. Add ground beef, then mix well. Shape mixture into four ½-inch-thick patties. Place patties in an 8x8x2-inch baking dish. Cover with waxed paper. Micro-cook on 100% power (HIGH) 4 to 6 minutes or till done, turning patties and rotating the dish a half-turn once.

2 large pita bread rounds, halved
4 lettuce leaves
Black olives (optional)

● Line each pita half with a lettuce leaf. Cut each burger in half. Place 2 burger halves in each pita half. Top with some of the avocado salsa. Garnish with black olives, if desired. Makes 4 servings.

Open-Face Reubens

3 slices rye *or* pumpernickel bread, toasted **3** tablespoons Thousand Island dressing	● Spread one side of each bread slice with dressing, then set aside.
½ pound thinly sliced corned beef **½** of an 8-ounce can (½ cup) sauerkraut, rinsed and drained **3** slices Swiss cheese **1** small tomato, thinly sliced Whole dill pickles (optional)	● On a nonmetal platter mound corned beef in 3 piles. Top with some sauerkraut. Micro-cook, uncovered, on 50% power (MEDIUM) 5 to 6 minutes or till heated through. Use a wide spatula to transfer to dressing side of bread slices. Top with cheese and tomato slices. Serve with dill pickles, if desired. Makes 3 servings.

Pictured, left to right on countertop:
Open-Face Reubens
Ham and Eggwiches
(see recipe, page 62)
Venetian Pizza Boats
(see recipe, page 67)
Fiesta Pitas
(see recipe, page 63)

Gyro Burgers

¼ cup crumbled feta cheese
3 tablespoons fine dry bread
   crumbs
¼ teaspoon dried oregano,
   crushed
⅛ teaspoon garlic powder
⅛ teaspoon pepper
1 pound ground lamb *or*
   beef

● In a mixing bowl combine feta cheese, bread crumbs, oregano, garlic powder, and pepper. Add meat, then mix well. Shape meat mixture into four ½-inch-thick oval-shaped patties.

   Place in a 10x6x2-inch baking dish. Cover with waxed paper. Micro-cook patties on 100% power (HIGH) 6 to 8 minutes or till done, turning patties and rotating the dish a half-turn once.

2 large pita bread rounds,
   halved
¼ cup dairy sour cream
1 cup shredded lettuce
1 small tomato, chopped
¼ cup chopped cucumber
¼ cup sliced pitted ripe
   olives

● Meanwhile, generously spread inside of pita halves with sour cream. Sprinkle some of the lettuce, tomato, and cucumber into each pita half. Place 1 patty in each pita half. Sprinkle with olives. Makes 4 servings.

To make a true-to-form Greek gyro (pronounced JEE-row or YEE-row) sandwich, you'd use pressed meat that's been grilled on a vertical rotisserie. Our version has the same robust seasonings as the real thing but comes in a burger that's easy to fix.

Open-Face Chili Sandwiches

½ pound ground beef
1 small onion, chopped
   (¼ cup)

● Crumble beef into a 2-quart casserole, then stir in onion. Micro-cook, covered, on 100% power (HIGH) 4½ to 5½ minutes or till beef is done and onion is tender, stirring once to break up meat.

1 8-ounce can red kidney
   beans, drained
1 8-ounce can tomato sauce
1½ teaspoons chili powder
¼ teaspoon salt
4 hamburger buns, split
1 cup shredded cheddar
   cheese (4 ounces)
1 cup shredded lettuce
   (optional)
¼ cup dairy sour cream
   (optional)

● Stir kidney beans, tomato sauce, chili powder, and salt into beef mixture. Micro-cook, covered, on 100% power (HIGH) about 4 minutes or till heated through, stirring once. Place 1 halved bun, cut side up, on each of 4 individual plates. Spoon some of the beef mixture atop both halves of each bun. Sprinkle with cheese. If desired, top with lettuce and sour cream. Makes 4 servings.

For the real chili enthusiast who craves chili in any shape or form, here's a mildly spicy version served on a bun.

Venetian Pizza Boats

Pictured on pages 64–65.

1 beaten egg 2 tablespoons fine dry bread crumbs ¼ teaspoon salt ⅛ teaspoon dried oregano, crushed Dash pepper ¼ pound ground beef	● In a medium mixing bowl combine egg, bread crumbs, salt, oregano, and pepper. Add ground beef, then mix well. Shape the meat mixture into 6 meatballs. Arrange meatballs in a circle in a 7- or 9-inch pie plate. Micro-cook, uncovered, on 100% power (HIGH) 3 to 5 minutes or till done, turning meatballs and rotating the pie plate a half-turn once. Drain.
1 medium zucchini, chopped (1 cup) 2 tablespoons chopped onion 1 tablespoon butter *or* margarine 1 small clove garlic, minced ½ cup pizza sauce	● In a small mixing bowl combine zucchini, onion, butter or margarine, and garlic. Micro-cook, uncovered, on 100% power (HIGH) 1½ to 2 minutes or till vegetables are crisp-tender, stirring once. Stir in pizza sauce. Micro-cook, uncovered, on 100% power (HIGH) 1 to 2 minutes or till sauce is heated through, stirring once.
2 individual French-style rolls 1 slice mozzarella cheese (1½ ounces) Pickled peppers (optional)	● To assemble sandwiches, cut and set aside a thin slice from top of each roll. Hollow bottoms of rolls, leaving ¼-inch shells. (Save excess bread for another use.) Place rolls in a nonmetal serving container. Place 3 meatballs in *each* hollowed roll. Cut cheese in half crosswise, then halve again diagonally to make 4 triangles. Spoon pizza sauce mixture over meatballs. Arrange 2 cheese triangles atop each meatball sandwich. Micro-cook, uncovered, on 100% power (HIGH) 1 to 1½ minutes or till cheese is melted. Garnish with pickled peppers, if desired. Makes 2 servings.

Mince garlic like a pro. First, place a clove on a cutting board. Then, using the flat side of a large knife, press down and forward to loosen the peel. Finally, remove the peel and finely chop the garlic, keeping the knife perpendicular to the cutting board.

Here's to one-dish meals where the dish is edible. On the next five pages, you'll find six vegetable favorites—all filled to the brim with savory stuffings.

Blue Cheese and Pork Peppers

1 tablespoon butter *or* margarine ¼ cup fine dry bread crumbs	● In a small bowl micro-cook butter or margarine, uncovered, on 100% power (HIGH) 30 to 40 seconds or till melted. Stir in bread crumbs, then set aside.
4 large green peppers 2 tablespoons water	● Cut tops from green peppers, then discard seeds and membranes. Chop enough of the tops to make ½ cup, then set aside. Place peppers, cut side up, and water in an 8x8x2-inch baking dish. Cover with vented clear plastic wrap. Micro-cook on 100% power (HIGH) 3 minutes. Drain and set aside.
1 pound ground pork 1 stalk celery, chopped 1 cup cooked rice 1 3-ounce package cream cheese, softened ½ of a 4-ounce package blue cheese, crumbled 2 tablespoons sliced pimiento, chopped	● Crumble pork into a 2-quart casserole, then stir in chopped pepper and celery. Micro-cook, covered, on 100% power (HIGH) 5 to 6 minutes or till pork is no longer pink, stirring once to break up pork. Drain off fat. Stir in rice, cream cheese, blue cheese, and pimiento.
	● Mound meat mixture into pepper shells. Cover with vented clear plastic wrap. Micro-cook on 100% power (HIGH) 4 to 5 minutes or till filling is hot and peppers are crisp-tender, rotating the dish once. Sprinkle with bread crumb mixture. Makes 4 servings.

If you like a good story as well as good food, credit the discovery of blue cheese to a shepherd boy who lost his cheese lunch in a cave. Legend has it that when he finally found his lunch, the cheese was streaked with mold, but delicious.

Tuna Melt Tomato

4 large tomatoes Salt	● Slice off stem end of tomatoes. Scoop out pulp and seeds to make a shell. Sprinkle inside of tomatoes with salt and invert onto paper towels.
1 stalk celery, chopped (½ cup) ¼ cup sliced green onion ¼ cup mayonnaise *or* salad dressing 1 teaspoon Dijon-style mustard 1 6½-ounce can tuna, drained and flaked 2 hard-cooked eggs, chopped 2 slices American cheese, halved diagonally	● Meanwhile, in a medium mixing bowl stir together celery, onion, mayonnaise or salad dressing, and mustard. Stir in tuna and eggs. Cover with vented clear plastic wrap. Micro-cook on 100% power (HIGH) 2½ to 3½ minutes or till heated through. Fill tomatoes with tuna mixture. Arrange in a circle in a 9-inch pie plate. Top each with cheese triangle. Micro-cook, uncovered, on 100% power (HIGH) 1 to 2 minutes or till cheese is melted. Makes 4 servings.

For a different twist on the tuna melt sandwich, try Tuna Melt Tomato. You stuff the hot tuna salad in a tomato shell and top it with cheese.

Tater Stroganoff

2 medium baking potatoes	● Scrub potatoes, then prick with a fork. In a shallow baking dish micro-cook potatoes, uncovered, on 100% power (HIGH) 6 to 8 minutes or till nearly done, rotating the dish once; set aside.
½ pound ground beef ½ cup shredded carrot ¼ cup sliced green onion ½ cup dairy sour cream 1 tablespoon all-purpose flour ¼ teaspoon salt ¼ cup milk	● Crumble beef into a 1½-quart casserole, then stir in carrot and onion. Micro-cook, covered, on 100% power (HIGH) 4½ to 5½ minutes or till done, stirring once to break up meat. Drain, then set aside. In a small bowl stir together sour cream, flour, and salt. Stir in milk. Stir into beef mixture. Micro-cook, uncovered, on 100% power (HIGH) 2 to 3 minutes or till thickened and bubbly, stirring every minute.
2 tablespoons dry white wine Paprika	● Meanwhile, with a hot pad gently roll potatoes under your hand to loosen pulp. Cut a lengthwise slit in each potato, then press ends and push up. Transfer potatoes to 2 individual dinner plates. Stir wine into beef mixture. Spoon atop potatoes. Sprinkle paprika atop. Makes 2 servings.

We borrowed the sour cream sauce for this potato fix-up from beef stroganoff—the classic main dish named for Count P. Stroganoff, a 19th-century Russian diplomat and gourmet, but more likely created by his French chef.

Lamb-Stuffed Eggplant

¾ **pound ground lamb** **1 medium onion, chopped** **(½ cup)**	● Crumble lamb into a 1½-quart casserole, then stir in onion. Micro-cook, covered, on 100% power (HIGH) 4½ to 5½ minutes or till lamb is done, stirring once to break up lamb. Drain off fat. Remove from casserole.

Back in the fifth century, the Chinese believed eggplant caused insanity. That's why they dubbed the purple or white pear-shape fruit "mad apple."

1 1- to 1¼-pound eggplant
1 tablespoon butter *or*
margarine
¼ cup fine dry bread crumbs
1 teaspoon Worcestershire
sauce
¼ teaspoon dried basil,
crushed
⅛ teaspoon dried rosemary,
crushed

● Meanwhile, halve eggplant lengthwise. Scoop out pulp leaving ¼-inch shell, then coarsely chop pulp.

In the 1½-quart casserole micro-cook pulp and butter or margarine, covered, on 100% power (HIGH) 2 to 4 minutes or till tender. Stir in lamb mixture, bread crumbs, Worcestershire sauce, basil, and rosemary. Spoon half of the lamb mixture into each eggplant shell.

¼ cup water
1 8-ounce can tomato-herb
sauce
Cilantro (optional)

● Place eggplant shells and water in an 8x8x2-inch baking dish. Cover with vented clear plastic wrap. Micro-cook on 100% power (HIGH) 5 to 7 minutes or till eggplant shell is fork-tender, rotating the dish once.

Cut each eggplant half in half again crosswise. Spoon tomato-herb sauce over eggplant. Micro-cook, uncovered, on 100% power (HIGH) about 1 minute or till sauce is heated through. Garnish with cilantro, if desired. Makes 4 servings.

Salmon-Stuffed Zucchini

1 beaten egg
1 teaspoon Worcestershire
    sauce
¾ teaspoon snipped
    dillweed *or* ¼ teaspoon
    dried dillweed
    Dash pepper
1 15½-ounce can salmon,
    drained, flaked, and
    skin and bones removed
½ cup cooked rice

● In a medium mixing bowl combine egg, Worcestershire sauce, dillweed, and pepper. Stir in salmon and cooked rice. Set aside.

Salmon-Stuffed Zucchini is a great choice for the dog days of summer. Dillweed adds light, refreshing summertime flavor. And using your microwave oven means you won't heat up the kitchen.

2 medium zucchini
    (5½ to 6 inches long)
1 small onion, chopped
    (¼ cup)

● Trim ends of zucchini, then halve lengthwise. Scrape out pulp leaving ¼-inch shells. Set shells aside. Finely chop zucchini pulp (should measure about ½ cup). In a medium bowl micro-cook chopped zucchini and onion, covered, on 100% power (HIGH) 1½ to 2 minutes or till onion is tender. Drain. Stir into salmon mixture.

● Place zucchini shells in a 12x7½x2-inch baking dish. Cover with vented clear plastic wrap. Micro-cook on 100% power (HIGH) 2 to 4 minutes or till zucchini are crisp-tender. Place some of the salmon mixture in each zucchini shell. Micro-cook, covered, on 100% power (HIGH) 4 to 6 minutes or till salmon mixture is heated through.

⅓ cup dairy sour cream
1 teaspoon Dijon-style
    mustard
    Dillweed (optional)

● For sauce, in a small bowl stir together sour cream and mustard. Spoon sauce over zucchini. Micro-cook, uncovered, on 100% power (HIGH) 30 to 60 seconds or till sauce is heated through. Garnish with dillweed, if desired. Makes 4 servings.

Acorn Squash with Pork

1 1-pound acorn squash	● Pierce squash with a meat fork several times, piercing all the way through to center. In a shallow baking dish microcook squash, uncovered, on 100% power (HIGH) 6 to 8 minutes or till squash can be pierced with a meat fork, turning squash over once. Set aside.
½ pound ground pork 2 tablespoons chopped onion	● Crumble pork into a 1-quart casserole, then stir in onion. Micro-cook, covered, on 100% power (HIGH) 4½ to 5½ minutes or till pork is no longer pink, stirring once to break up pork. Drain.
1 small cooking apple, peeled, cored, and chopped (½ cup) ¼ cup raisins ¼ cup coarsley chopped walnuts *or* pecans 2 tablespoons tomato sauce ¼ teaspoon salt ⅛ teaspoon ground cinnamon Cinnamon (optional)	● Stir in apple, raisins, nuts, tomato sauce, salt, and the ⅛ teaspoon cinnamon. Halve squash lengthwise, then discard seeds. Scoop out pulp, leaving ¼-inch shells, and chop pulp. Stir pulp into sausage mixture. Spoon into shells. Return shells to the baking dish. Cover with vented clear plastic wrap. Micro-cook on 100% power (HIGH) 4 to 5 minutes or till heated through. Sprinkle with additional cinnamon, if desired. Makes 2 servings.

Believe us, it's worth the little time it takes to pierce vegetables such as potatoes and acorn squash before microwave cooking. Venting allows the steam to escape during cooking and prevents the vegetable from exploding all over your oven.

Get in Step

Your microwave oven is a real time saver, but you may need to rearrange the work flow so you're ready when your meal-in-one dish is. Instead of setting the table and preparing a salad or dessert while your one-dish meal cooks, do these tasks first. And be sure everybody is ready to come to the table. Once you pop your one-dish meal in the microwave oven it won't be long before dinner is ready.

Polenta-Topped Beef

1 **cup cold water** ⅓ **cup yellow cornmeal** ¼ **teaspoon salt** ½ **cup shredded American cheese (2 ounces)**	● For polenta, place water in a medium mixing bowl, then stir in cornmeal and salt. Micro-cook, uncovered, on 100% power (HIGH) about 3 minutes or till water boils and mixture is very thick and smooth, stirring every minute. Stir in cheese and set aside.
1 **medium onion, chopped (½ cup)** 2 **tablespoons butter or margarine** 1 **clove garlic, minced**	● In a 1½-quart casserole micro-cook onion, butter or margarine, and garlic, uncovered, on 100% power (HIGH) 2 to 3 minutes or till onion is tender.
1 **tablespoon all-purpose flour** 2 **cups cubed cooked beef** 1 **12-ounce can whole kernel corn with sweet peppers, drained** 1 **8-ounce can tomatoes, cut up** ¼ **teaspoon dried oregano, crushed**	● Stir in flour, then stir in beef, corn, *undrained* tomatoes, and oregano. Micro-cook, uncovered, on 100% power (HIGH) 6 to 8 minutes or till thickened and bubbly, stirring every 2 minutes. Using a large star tip and pastry bag, pipe polenta in a lattice design over beef mixture. Or, spoon polenta atop. Micro-cook, uncovered, on 100% power (HIGH) 3 to 5 minutes or till polenta is heated through, rotating the dish a half-turn after 2 minutes. Let stand, uncovered, 5 minutes. Makes 4 servings.

Puff-Topped Pork

1 **9-ounce package frozen cut green beans**	● Thaw green beans (see tip, page 17), then set aside.
1 **medium onion, chopped (½ cup)**	In a 2-quart casserole micro-cook onion, carrot, and butter or margarine, covered, on 100% power (HIGH) 2 to 3 minutes or till onion is tender. Stir in flour, thyme, and pepper. Stir in milk and chicken broth all at once. Micro-cook, uncovered, on 100% power (HIGH) 5 to 7 minutes or till thickened and bubbly, stirring every minute.
1 **carrot, shredded (½ cup)**	
¼ **cup butter** *or* **margarine**	
¼ **cup all-purpose flour**	
½ **teaspoon dried thyme, crushed**	
Dash pepper	
1 **cup milk**	
1 **cup chicken broth**	

2 **cups cubed, cooked pork**	● Stir in green beans, pork, cheese, and mushrooms. Micro-cook, covered, on 100% power (HIGH) 8 to 10 minutes or till beans are crisp-tender, stirring once. Keep covered and set aside.
½ **cup shredded American cheese (2 ounces)**	
1 **2½-ounce jar sliced mushrooms, drained**	

3 **egg yolks**	● For topper, in a small mixer bowl beat egg yolks on high speed of an electric mixer about 5 minutes or till thick and lemon colored.
½ **cup all-purpose flour**	
2 **tablespoons grated Parmesan cheese**	In a small bowl stir together flour, cheese, and baking powder. Combine milk and oil. Stir flour mixture and milk mixture alternately into beaten egg yolks. Stir in parsley. Wash the beaters.
1 **teaspoon baking powder**	
½ **cup milk**	
1 **tablespoon cooking oil**	
2 **tablespoons snipped parsley**	

3 **egg whites**	● In a large mixer bowl beat egg whites till stiff peaks form. Fold yolk mixture into egg whites. Carefully spoon atop pork mixture, then sprinkle with paprika.
Paprika	
	Micro-cook, uncovered, on 50% power (MEDIUM) 8 to 10 minutes or till topper is done, rotating the dish a half-turn once. Let stand 5 minutes before serving. Makes 6 servings.

A soufflé-like topper makes Puff-Topped Pork so good it's hard to believe it starts with leftovers. To test the doneness of the topper, just insert a wooden toothpick into the center. When it comes out clean, your casserole is finished.

Oriental Chicken Pilaf

2 cups loose-pack frozen mixed beans, broccoli, mushrooms, and red peppers 1 cup water ½ teaspoon instant chicken bouillon granules 1 cup quick-cooking rice	● In a 2-quart casserole micro-cook vegetables, water, and bouillon granules, uncovered, on 100% power (HIGH) 7 to 8 minutes or till boiling. Stir in rice, then let stand, covered, 5 to 8 minutes or till rice is tender and liquid is absorbed.
2 cups cubed, cooked chicken 2 tablespoons dry sherry 2 tablespoons soy sauce ⅛ teaspoon pepper 2 tablespoons cold water 1 teaspoon cornstarch ¼ cup unsalted peanuts, chopped (optional)	● Stir chicken, sherry, soy sauce, and pepper into rice mixture. Stir together water and cornstarch. Stir into chicken-and-rice mixture. Micro-cook, covered, on 100% power (HIGH) 3 to 5 minutes or till thickened and bubbly, stirring every minute. Micro-cook 30 seconds more. If desired, sprinkle peanuts atop. Serves 4.

Your best rice bet for microwave cooking is the quick-cooking variety. Long grain rice is more likely to bubble up and make a mess unless you cook it at lower power settings for a longer time.

Bulgur Beef

1¼ cups hot water 1 teaspoon instant beef bouillon granules ¾ cup bulgur wheat	● In a 2-quart casserole micro-cook the water and beef bouillon granules, covered, on 100% power (HIGH) about 6 minutes or till boiling. Stir in bulgur wheat and let stand about 15 minutes or till liquid is absorbed.
1 10-ounce package frozen peas ½ cup sliced green onion 2 tablespoons soy sauce ½ teaspoon finely shredded lemon peel 1 clove garlic, minced	● Stir in peas, onion, soy sauce, lemon peel, and garlic. Micro-cook, covered, on 100% power (HIGH) about 3 minutes or till peas are tender, stirring once.
1½ cups cubed, cooked beef ½ cup peanuts Lemon wedges (optional)	● Stir in beef and peanuts. Micro-cook, covered, on 100% power (HIGH) 3 to 4 minutes or till heated through, stirring once. Garnish with lemon wedges, if desired. Makes 4 servings.

Look for bulgur wheat in your local supermarket or health food store. If you can't find it, substitute cracked wheat cereal instead and continue as directed.

Ham and Potato Casserole

1	12-ounce package frozen shredded hash brown potatoes
3	tablespoons butter *or* margarine
	Dash pepper
1	cup milk
1½	teaspoons minced dried onion

● Thaw potatoes (see tip, page 17). Drain well. In a medium bowl micro-cook butter or margarine, uncovered, on 100% power (HIGH) 40 to 50 seconds or till melted. Stir in potatoes and pepper. Press into bottom of a 9-inch pie plate. Micro-cook, uncovered, on 100% power (HIGH) 10 minutes, rotating the dish once. Meanwhile, combine milk and onion; set aside.

2	tablespoons butter *or* margarine
2	tablespoons all-purpose flour
1	teaspoon instant chicken bouillon granules
½	teaspoon Worcestershire sauce

● In a 4-cup measure micro-cook butter or margarine, uncovered, on 100% power (HIGH) 40 to 50 seconds or till melted. Stir in flour, bouillon granules, and Worcestershire sauce. Stir in milk mixture. Micro-cook, uncovered, on 100% power (HIGH) 2 to 3 minutes or till bubbly, stirring every minute.

½	cup shredded American cheese (2 ounces)
1	10-ounce package frozen peas
½	pound diced fully cooked ham (1½ cups)
½	of a 3-ounce can french-fried onions

● Stir in cheese. Micro-cook, uncovered, on 100% power (HIGH) about 30 seconds or till melted. Stir in peas.

Layer ham atop potato mixture. Pour pea mixture atop ham. Micro-cook, uncovered, on 100% power (HIGH) 10 to 12 minutes or till peas are tender, rotating the dish twice. Top with onions. Micro-cook, uncovered, on 100% power (HIGH) 1 minute. Serves 4.

Fill 'em up. This ham-and-vegetable-filled potato pie is just the thing to feed a hungry family of four.

Hash Brown Hash

1 small onion, chopped
   (¼ cup)
1 tablespoon butter *or*
   margarine

● In a 1-quart casserole micro-cook onion and butter or margarine, covered, on 100% power (HIGH) 1 to 1½ minutes or till onion is tender.

1 cup frozen fried hash
   brown potatoes
1 cup finely chopped
   cooked beef
2 tablespoons snipped
   parsley (optional)
2 teaspoons Worcestershire
   sauce
⅛ teaspoon salt
⅛ teaspoon pepper
1 5⅓-ounce can (⅔ cup)
   evaporated milk
2 teaspoons all-purpose
   flour

● Stir in potatoes; beef; parsley, if desired; Worcestershire sauce; salt; and pepper. Micro-cook, covered, on 100% power (HIGH) about 3 minutes or till heated through. Combine milk and flour, then stir into meat mixture. Micro-cook, uncovered, on 100% power (HIGH) about 3 minutes or till thickened and bubbly, stirring every minute. Serves 2.

For centuries cooks have combined leftover beef and potatoes to make a quick-and-easy one-dish meal. This recipe qualifies as a hash because the meat is chopped, not ground.

Quick-as-a-Wink Chicken a la King

1 10¾-ounce can
   condensed cream of
   mushroom soup
⅓ cup milk
2 tablespoons dry sherry
¼ teaspoon pepper
2 cups diced cooked
   chicken
1½ cups frozen peas
2 tablespoons sliced
   pimiento, chopped
   (optional)
   Toast points

● In a 1½-quart casserole stir together soup, milk, sherry, and pepper. Stir in chicken, peas, and, if desired, pimiento. Micro-cook, covered, on 100% power (HIGH) 7 to 8 minutes or till heated through, stirring twice. Serve over toast points. Makes 4 servings.

Cooked poultry doesn't keep long. After a big chicken dinner, plan to use any leftovers within two days. If that's a problem, freeze the chicken in a moisture- and vaporproof wrap. That way you can keep it for about a month.

Index

A-B

Acorn Squash with Pork, 73
Beef
    Beef and Bean Paprikash, 33
    Beef and Cabbage, 49
    Beef and Vegetable
        Carbonnade, 17
    Beef Florentine, 61
    Beer-Sauced Meatballs, 34
    Blaze-of-Glory Chili, 8
    Bulgur Beef, 76
    Burgundy Beef and Asparagus, 48
    Chili-Mac Casserole, 22
    Choose-a-Dumpling Beef Stew, 30
    Fiesta Pitas, 63
    Freezer Beef Base, 42
    Hash Brown Hash, 78
    Meatballs with French Onion
        Sauce, 51
    Mexican Corn Bread
        Casserole, 35
    No-Measure Beef Stew, 40
    Open-Face Chili Sandwiches, 67
    Open-Face Reubens, 64
    Peppered Beef, 25
    Polenta-Topped Beef, 74
    Sauerbraten Meatballs, 51
    Spaghetti Squash and
        Meatballs, 50
    Taco Casserole, 15
    Tater Stroganoff, 70
    Vegetable Beef Soup, 46
    Venetian Pizza Boats, 67
    Zesty Beef Stroganoff, 12
Beer-Sauced Meatballs, 34
Blaze-of-Glory Chili, 8
Blue Cheese and Pork Peppers, 69
Bouillabaisse, 60
Broccoli and Veal Bundles, 54
Bulgur Beef, 76
Burgundy Beef and Asparagus, 48

C

Cake, Dutch Apple, 59
Carbonnade, Beef and Vegetable, 17
Carrot Dumplings, 28

Casseroles
    Chili-Mac Casserole, 22
    Cock-a-Noodle Casserole, 35
    Corny Calico Casseroles, 20
    Creamed Chickaroni
        Casserole, 22
    Greek Lamb and Cheese
        Casserole, 24
    Ham and Potato Casserole, 77
    It's-a-Spicy-Spaghetti Casserole, 8
    Mexican Corn Bread
        Casserole, 35
    Salami-Vegetable Bake, 37
    Salmon-Noodle Bake, 27
    Taco Casserole, 15
Cheddar Dumplings, 28
Cheese
    Blue Cheese and Pork
        Peppers, 69
    Cheddar Dumplings, 28
    Chilies and Cheese Rice, 21
    Greek Lamb and Cheese
        Casserole, 24
    Ham-and-Rye Strata, 23
    Macaroni and Beer Cheese, 14
    Shrimp with Gruyère Sauce, 53
Chicken
    Chicken à l'Orange, 58
    Chicken Couscous, 16
    Chicken Enchiladas, 44
    Chicken Paella, 9
    Cock-a-Noodle Casserole, 35
    Creamed Chickaroni
        Casserole, 22
    Creamy Chicken and Rice, 38
    Creole-Style Chicken, 32
    Curried Chicken and Rice, 45
    Freezer Chicken Base, 42
    Oriental Chicken Pilaf, 76
    Quick-as-a-Wink Chicken a la
        King, 78
Chili, Blaze-of-Glory, 8
Chilies and Cheese Rice, 21
Chili-Mac Casserole, 22
Choose-a-Dumpling Beef Stew, 30
Cock-a-Noodle Casserole, 35
Corn Bread Dumplings, 28
Corny Calico Casseroles, 20
Couscous, Chicken, 16
Creamed Chickaroni Casserole, 22

Creamy Chicken and Rice, 38
Creole-Style Chicken, 32
Curried Chicken and Rice, 45

D-F

Dumplings
    Carrot Dumplings, 28
    Cheddar Dumplings, 28
    Choose-a-Dumpling Beef Stew, 30
    Corn Bread Dumplings, 28
    Herbed Dumplings, 28
Dutch Apple Cake, 59
Easy Cassoulet, 36
Enchiladas, Chicken, 44
Faux Polish Hunter's Stew, 13
Fiesta Pitas, 63
Fish and Seafood
    Bouillabaisse, 60
    Chicken Paella, 9
    Salmon-Noodle Bake, 27
    Salmon-Stuffed Zucchini, 72
    Shortcut Gumbo, 39
    Shrimp with Gruyère Sauce, 53
    Tuna Melt Tomato, 70
Freezer Base Recipes
    Beef and Cabbage, 49
    Burgundy Beef and Asparagus, 48
    Chicken Enchiladas, 44
    Curried Chicken and Rice, 45
    Freezer Beef Base, 42
    Freezer Chicken Base, 42
    Freezer Meatball Base, 43
    Sauerbraten Meatballs, 51
    Spaghetti Squash and
        Meatballs, 50

G-M

Greek Lamb and Cheese
    Casserole, 24
Gumbo, Shortcut, 39
Gyro Burgers, 67
Ham and Eggwiches, 62
Ham and Potato Casserole, 77
Ham-and-Rye Strata, 23
Hash Brown Hash, 78
Herbed Dumplings, 28
It's-a-Spicy-Spaghetti Casserole, 8
Knackwurst in Beer, 63

Lamb
  Greek Lamb and Cheese
    Casserole, 24
  Gyro Burgers, 67
  Lamb-Stuffed Eggplant, 70
  Ye New Irish Stew, 12
Lasagna, Zucchini, 10
Macaroni and Beer Cheese, 14
Manicotti, Pork-and-Spinach, 31
Meatballs
  Beer-Sauced Meatballs, 34
  Meatballs with French Onion
    Sauce, 51
  Sauerbraten Meatballs, 51
  Spaghetti Squash and
    Meatballs, 50
Mexican Corn Bread Casserole, 35
Minestrone, Quick, 38

N-R

No-Measure Beef Stew, 40
Open-Face Chili Sandwiches, 67
Open-Face Reubens, 64
Oriental Chicken Pilaf, 76
Paella, Chicken, 9
Paprikash, Beef and Bean, 33
Pasta
  Chili-Mac Casserole, 22
  Cock-a-Noodle Casserole, 35
  Creamed Chickaroni
    Casserole, 22
  Greek Lamb and Cheese
    Casserole, 24
  It's-a-Spicy-Spaghetti Casserole, 8
  Macaroni and Beer Cheese, 14
  Pork-and-Spinach Manicotti, 31
  Quick Minestrone, 38
  Salmon-Noodle Bake, 27
  Sausage and Apple Pastitsio, 52
Pastitsio, Sausage and Apple, 52
Peppered Beef, 25
Polenta-Topped Beef, 74
Pork
  Acorn Squash with Pork, 73
  Blue Cheese and Pork
    Peppers, 69
  Freezer Meatball Base, 43

Pork (continued)
  Meatballs with French Onion
    Sauce, 51
  Pork-and-Spinach Manicotti, 31
  Pork Chops and Rice Dijon, 55
  Puff-Topped Pork, 75
  Sauerbraten Meatballs, 51
  Spaghetti Squash and
    Meatballs, 50
  Sweet-and-Sour-Sauced Pork, 19
Puff-Topped Pork, 75
Quick-as-a-Wink Chicken a la
  King, 78
Quick Minestrone, 38
Reubens, Open-Face, 64

S

Salad, Tarragon Spinach, 59
Salami-Vegetable Bake, 37
Salmon-Noodle Bake, 27
Salmon-Stuffed Zucchini, 72
Sandwiches
  Fiesta Pitas, 63
  Gyro Burgers, 67
  Ham and Eggwiches, 62
  Knackwurst in Beer, 63
  Open-Face Chili Sandwiches, 67
  Open-Face Reubens, 64
  Venetian Pizza Boats, 67
Sauerbraten Meatballs, 51
Sausages
  Chicken Paella, 9
  Corny Calico Casseroles, 20
  Easy Cassoulet, 36
  Faux Polish Hunter's Stew, 13
  It's-a-Spicy-Spaghetti Casserole, 8
  Knackwurst in Beer, 63
  Salami-Vegetable Bake, 37
  Sausage and Apple Pastitsio, 52
  Shepherd's Pie, 41
  Zucchini Lasagna, 10
Shepherd's Pie, 41
Shortcut Gumbo, 39
Shrimp with Gruyère Sauce, 53
Soups
  Quick Minestrone, 38
  Shortcut Gumbo, 39
  Vegetable Beef Soup, 46
Spaghetti Squash and Meatballs, 50

Stews
  Bouillabaisse, 60
  Choose-a-Dumpling Beef Stew, 30
  Faux Polish Hunter's Stew, 13
  No-Measure Beef Stew, 40
  Ye New Irish Stew, 12
Strata, Ham-and-Rye, 23
Stroganoff, Tater, 70
Stroganoff, Zesty Beef, 12
Sweet-and-Sour-Sauced Pork, 19

T-Z

Taco Casserole, 15
Tarragon Spinach Salad, 59
Tater Stroganoff, 70
Tuna Melt Tomato, 70
Veal Bundles, Broccoli and, 54
Vegetable Beef Soup, 46
Venetian Pizza Boats, 67
White Wine Spritzers, 58
Ye New Irish Stew, 12
Zesty Beef Stroganoff, 12
Zucchini Lasagna, 10

Tips

Eggs That Excel, 62
Finishing Touches, 49
Freezer Lowdown, 44
Freezer Wrap-Ups, 43
Get in Step, 73
Letting Off Steam, 21
Microwave Wattage, 6
Organize for Speedy Suppers, 24
Second-String Substitutions, 36
Thawing Vegetables in a Hurry, 17
Variable Power, 6
Your Microwave Cookware, 7